Small Group Discussion Topics for Korean Students

Small Group Discussion Topics for Korean Students

By Jack Martire

Published by **Pusan National University Press**

PRINTING HISTORY

First Edition: March 1990
Second Printing: February 1992
Third Printing: January 1994
Fourth Printing: August 1995
Second Edition: June 1999
Fifth Printing: July 1996
Sixth Printing: March 1997
Seventh Printing: June 1999
Eighth Printing: December 2001
Third Edition: September 2002
Fourth Edition: September 2003
Ninth Printing: August 2003
Tenth Printing: February 2005
Eleventh Printing: August 2006
Fifth Edition: October 2007
Twelfth Printing: January 2008
Thirteenth Printing: April 2009
Sixth Edition: February 2011
Seventh Edition: October 2013

For information address: Pusan National University Press
2, Busandaehak-ro 63beon-gil, Geumjeong-gu, Busan 609-735
Republic of Korea (KR)
Tel: (8251) 510-1932
Fax: (8251) 512-7812

Questions or comments pertaining to the contents should be addressed to the author via email at: martire05@gmail.com

Price : 13,000 won

ISBN 978-89-7316-452-3 03740
Reg. No. 11-2, Sept. 10, 1992

Printed in the Republic of Korea

Jack Martire holds an M.Ed. in English education from Pennsylvania State University and has undertaken additional graduate studies in International Affairs and Asian languages at the University of Pittsburgh and language centers in Japan and Thailand.

He has studied 9 languages but considers himself most comfortable in Japanese, Korean, and Thai. His resume includes teaching h.s. English for the US Department of Defense and serving as US Customs inspector on the US/Canadian border. The bulk of his professional career, however, has been spent teaching and directing English language programs in Japan and Korea. Honolulu is home, but he currently resides in Bangkok, where he is researching a Thai version of SGDT.

Prof. Martire has been on the staff of a number of public and private universities in Korea, including Pusan National University, Sogang University, and the Korea Maritime University. He published the first edition of Small Group Discussion Topics for Korean Students in 1990, before directing the English language training program for the Kolon Corporation Training Center in Yongin for 8 years.

Prof. Martire believes that fluency is best acquired not through textbook dialogues, memorization, and classroom drills with which students cannot identify but through situations requiring practical use of the language, similar to the way that babies learn to talk. Asked to discuss subjects with which they are already familiar, students tend to focus on the content of their discussions and lose sight of the fact that they are primarily learning a foreign language.

Contact the author: martire05@gmail.com

Other books by Jack Martire

1. ***Small Group Discussion Topics for University Students*** Political, economic, environmental, and social issues facing the world in the early 21sth Century, 4th Edition, PNU Press, 2011.
2. ***Small Group Discussion Topics for Korean Teenagers*** Topics important to Korean high school students presented in Conversational North American English, (with Korean translations) PNU Press, 2013.

Small Group Discussion Topics for Korean Students

CONTENTS

A new twist in the online sex trade—older women hunting boys. 9

Demographic shift— By 2020 49% of all children in rural Korea will be bi-racial. 21

Korean racism exposed—how many non-white English teachers are there in Korea? 33

K-pop has Korean Fever sweeping the world—how long can it last? 45

Expensive, imported luxury goods—Koreans can't seem to get enough. 53

Love Hotels—just convenient places to cheat on one's spouse? 57

CONTENTS

INTRODUCTION

THE SGDT SERIES

The Small Group Discussion Topics series for university and high school students by Jack Martire is the single most widely used English conversation teaching tool in Korean universities, high schools and private English language institutes. Since the first edition was published in 1990 all three books in the series have steadily gained in popularity, collectively appearing on the Korean textbook bestseller list consistently since 1999.

Contributing to the popularity of the SGDT series has been its uniqueness as the only set of English conversation teaching materials designed specifically for Korean learners.

THE SEVENTH EDITION

This seventh edition of Small Group Discussion Topics for Korean Students is intended for students at the intermediate or advanced levels of English proficiency. The book contains 40 discussion topics which focus on political, economic, environmental and social issues of interest to Koreans in the early 21st century.

Some topics are more difficult to discuss than others since they require the use of more specialized vocabulary. For this reason teachers and group leaders should use discretion when assigning topics, keeping in mind the ability level of their particular group of students. They should also consider the complexity of language required to discuss those topics effectively. Assigning a topic whose discussion would require a level of proficiency greater than the students possess will tempt them to resort to the use of their native language.

THE TOPICS

Most topics deal with the normal everyday concerns of people everywhere, while others are clearly out of the range of normal daily conversation. The thing that all topics have in common is that they are highly controversial and invite argument to defend one's point of view. What could be more boring than a discussion during which everybody agrees with everyone else on everything?

A word of caution: Some of the topics in this book contain content that could be viewed as critical of Korean society and may offend ultra-nationalistic students who would prefer to focus solely on the positive aspects of Korean life while ignoring the negative. They may particularly resent a foreign author writing about such sensitive issues concerning their country.

However, Koreans themselves, and not the author, actually chose the subject matter for this book because every topic in this book had already been written about in Korean English-language newspapers before the decision was made to include it.

THE ARTICLES

Each discussion topic is introduced by a 3-part article which focuses on one aspect of the problem or issue. In general, reading 1 provides background, reading 2 outlines the current state or condition, and reading 3 focuses on the future and/or solutions. Dividing the readings up into short segments makes it easier for students to organize their thoughts in preparation for the discussions that follow.

ENGLISH USAGE

North American spoken English usage and not the type of expressions normally found in English prose is used in the articles. This means that the grammar may not always be "by the book". Just as native English speakers often ignore the rules, no attempt to be grammatically perfect is made here either. "It's me" may not be acceptable grammatically, but one would be hard pressed to find many native speakers who would say "It is I".

THE DISCUSSION QUESTIONS

The questions that follow each article are not reading comprehension questions. Instead, they refer to the discussion topic and only make references to the article, assuming however, that it has been read and understood. It is important that the articles are not skipped over because there are references in the discussion questions to statements contained in the articles, and students are asked to agree, disagree, or elaborate.

VOCABULARY ENHANCEMENT

Because the readings expose students to a wide range of issues they are an effective tool for helping students develop a well-rounded speaking vocabulary. Some of the units expose students to subjects they may know little or nothing about, in which case the readings also serve as a learning tool.

Because space is limited, the readings can provide only a brief introduction to the topics, just enough to stimulate students to discuss. To find out more, students will have to research more deeply on their own. The purpose of the readings is not to provide a comprehensive treatment of the issues but simply to stimulate discussion.

SKEPTICAL STUDENTS

I have been accused more than once by skeptics of having used a Korean ghost writer to write this book. Some Koreans can't seem to conceive of any foreigner being intimate enough with Korean history and culture to write on topics like the ones included here. One brash young man wrote to ask, *"Who really wrote this book? Did you even read it!?"*

Well, before anybody writes to ask if I have read the book, let me state unequivocally that I not only read it but wrote every word without the help of even one Korean.

Kwangju, May 1980

I arrived in Korea three months before the Kwangju riot of 1980, long before today's college students were even born. So I lived through the tumultuous years that followed under the dictatorships of Chun Doo Hwan and Roh Tae Woo.

I watched first hand as Korea transformed itself from a country still in the throes of the Cold War with a nighttime curfew still in effect, into the world class nation that it is today. It is no exaggeration to say that I know more about recent Korean history than the students using my books because I experienced it first hand while they got it second hand.

While in Korea I lived among Koreans, and did things that foreigners never do...such as design and build a house in a rural village surrounded by rice fields. That experience taught me all I ever wanted to know about how Koreans thought, lived, and conducted business.

I lived in 5 different Busan "dongs" over a period of 13 years and in 3 Kyeonggi-do communities over a period of 5 years, half of them rural. So the suggestion that I must have had help from a Korean in writing this book is truly laughable.

Jack Martire

Author Jack Martire's solar house being constructed in Busan's Kangdong-dong in the summer of 1983, and the completed house as it appeared in 1987, the same year that massive street demonstrations forced military dictator Chun Doo Hwan from power.

HOW TO USE THIS BOOK

OBJECTIVES

The material in this book can be used in a variety of ways, depending on the type of discussion group, the general purpose of the class or group, and the English ability of the students. Although the original purpose for putting the book together was to provide discussion topics for English clubs and other small groups of unsupervised students outside the classroom, the material can be used even more effectively under the direction of an instructor.

To ensure that students get the most out of their discussions, it is imperative that only English be permitted throughout. No use of the native language should be permitted under any circumstances. If students are not proficient enough in English to follow this basic rule, then this book is not for them. Allowing students to use their native language defeats the purpose of the book, which is to have students develop ease in conversing in English on a wide variety of topics.

FORMING THE GROUPS

I. Group Size. If the instructor is confident that the students can conduct a discussion all in English completely on their own, he or she should break up the class into groups of between four and six students each. Any more than this number reduces the amount of time that any one student can speak, and any fewer lessens the potential that differing opinions will occur. Obviously, the most interesting discussions will occur when the speakers disagree with one another, so it's essential that there be enough students in the group to allow that to happen.

II. Mix up the Levels. Within any class or group the English speaking ability of the members will vary, and so instructors or group leaders should be careful not to assign all the best speakers in the class to one group and all the poorer speakers to another. Students should never be allowed to choose their own groups because they will most likely choose their friends, who may have the same English ability as their own.

Ability levels should be mixed so that better speakers can not only keep the discussions moving forward but also provide an incentive for students with lesser ability to keep up. Students who are less confident in speaking in English will be less tempted to use their native language if they are in the company of better speakers than if all the other students in the group have just as much trouble speaking English as they do. This point cannot be over-emphasized.

THE INSTRUCTOR'S ROLE

I. Read the article together. Regardless of the English proficiency level of the students, the instructor should first introduce the topic by taking ten minutes or so to go over the introductory article with the students. A good way of doing this is to have different students take turns in reading aloud, after which the teacher then reads the entire article while students follow along. It's important that the teacher takes the time to do this to ensure that the students learn the pronunciation of words or expressions they may be seeing for the first time.

Even though the questions that follow the articles are not reading comprehension questions, a teacher-led introduction stimulates interest in the topic and increases students' motivation to discuss it.

II. Explain new vocabulary. Terms that students may be unfamiliar with are underlined and then explained separately after the readings, but some students may need further clarification. Students can't practice using new words unless they're sure of what they mean.

III. Move around. After the introduction, and with the students in their small groups scattered around the room, the instructor should play the role of observer or occasional participant in the discussions. He or she should move around from group to group, interjecting a question or comment from time to time to stimulate discussion but never assuming a lead role. Students will be all too willing to let the teacher take over and do most of the talking, but don't allow that to happen. If that even begins to occur, get up and move to another group.

IV. Lend a helping hand. The instructor's role is not to actually participate in the group discussions but only to assist students who are having difficulty expressing their thoughts in English. If there is a sense that things are going well without teacher input, students should be left to fend for themselves. Only when there is a lull in the discussion or when teachers sense that important points are not being covered adequately should they intercede.

V. Overlook bad grammar. Teachers may be tempted to correct students every time they hear someone utter an ungrammatical phrase or sentence, but they should refrain from cutting in. Interrupting students to correct their grammar is a no-win situation since it shatters the momentum the students had going in the discussion and makes the students who are corrected afraid to open their mouths. All that really matters is that students are practicing English; the time for correction will come later.

VI. Discussion procedure. The success of any small group discussion is dependent on each student responding to each question. In a classroom situation, one student would answer one question and a different student would answer the next question. However, that won't work in this situation because having only one answer per question doesn't allow any kind of disagreement or differing opinion to arise. It is only by having 5 or 6 responses to the same question that a disagreement, and thus a genuine discussion, can occur.

WRAP-UP SESSION

When the instructor senses that the topic has been sufficiently talked out and all the important points have been covered he or she should bring all the students back into one large group again for a wrap-up session lasting another 10 minutes or so.

The primary purpose of this teacher-led session is to summarize some of the important points that came out during the discussions. During this session students should be given a chance to restate for the whole group some of the points and opinions they stated during their small group discussions.

The wrap-up session is the time to make grammatical corrections, now that the teacher is back in control of the discussion. When students are not able to express a thought in correct English, the instructor, as role model, should paraphrase correctly what they had wanted to say but couldn't.

This is the single most effective and most appreciated learning tool in the development of fluency for any language learner—having a native speaker articulate a thought that came from his or her very own head.

CLASS TIME TO ALLOT FOR DISCUSSIONS

Experience has shown that if the above procedures are followed, students at the intermediate levels of fluency or higher can carry on a discussion on any topic in this book for 35 minutes or more. Assuming that the reading and comprehension period that precedes the small group discussions takes 10 or 15 minutes, and the wrap-up session takes another 10 minutes, the minimum time needed to cover a topic adequately is about one class period to an hour. This is a modest estimate since depending on the topic, student level of English proficiency, and the amount of interest in the topic, a small group discussion period alone could go on an hour or longer.

If the class is teacher-led, the teacher can use his or her discretion as to when to begin the wrap-up session, according to time limitation. If the discussion group is an English club meeting with a group leader students will naturally decide for themselves when to end their discussions.

ENGLISH CLUBS AND STUDY GROUPS

The original purpose of the SGDT series back in 1990 was to provide discussion materials for English clubs and study groups, so it is not necessary to have a native speaker instructor to use the books. The club president or group leader can easily assume the role of instructor and divide up the group into the suggested number of members, keeping in mind the need to mix up the ability levels of the students.

Each group should have a group leader, whose primary responsibility is to make sure that every student expresses his or her opinion on each question.

UNIT 1 Korea Then and Now

Society

Seoul on a normal traffic day under a pollution-free sky in 1988.

Much has been written about Korea's rags to riches story and how much the country has changed in the past few decades, but Koreans under the age of 40 can't relate to that. If it were possible to rewind the clock to just before the 1988 Seoul Olympics, today's young generation would be shocked at what they would find—a military dictatorship government, a drab and dark environment, very few cars on the roads and no modern communication devices. Half of the Korean population had no telephones in the 1980s.

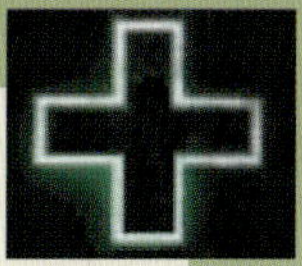

Until 1987 the only neon signs permitted in Korea were small neon crosses on churches or pharmacies. Any other use of neon was banned. The ban on neon was partly to save electricity and partly to protect the country from possible nighttime air attacks from the north.

There were only four TV channels in the 80s, and they all showed the same kinds of programs. The first 20-25 minutes of every news broadcast were devoted to images and news about Chun Doo Hwan or Roh Tae Woo, the military dictators of that period. All TV broadcasting was in black and white.

A typical Korean street scene in 1980. Count the cars.

Vocabulary

- **rags...story**: very fast economic development
- **relate to:** can understand it well because of having experienced it
- **drab**: not colorful, boring
- **device**: some kind of tool made for a particular purpose
- **pharmacies**: stores where they sell medicine and drugs
- **broadcast**: put on radio or TV

A pharmacy in the UK

These phone booths were once **jammed** with people.

Korea's first fast food chain, since 1987

Keeping appointments and contacting people in 1988's Korea was a nightmare. There were no mobile phones or pocket pagers, so if you were sitting in a taxi or a bus stuck in traffic you had no way to let the other person that you'd be late. Missed appointments were a way of life in the '80s.

> "Missed appointments were a way of life in the 1980s."

Many people didn't even have home phones because there was a long waiting list to have a phone installed. So the only way to contact anybody was by public pay phone, hoping that they would be at home.

There were always long lines of people waiting at public phone booths. Today they stand idle because everyone has a cell phone.

Today's under 30 crowd might starve to death if they had to live in the 1980s. That's because there were no fast food restaurants in Korea. They didn't start to enter Korea until 1987, one year before the 88 Seoul Olympics, and that was primarily for the benefit of the foreigners who would be visiting Korea. Today every conceivable foreign fast food chain plus some Korean ones can be found all over Korea.

Very few apartment buildings in the 1980s were higher than 12 stories because that's as high as fire truck ladders could reach. The ones being built today are 30- to 70-story skyscrapers, and most Koreans are not afraid to live in them.

The 69-story Samsung Tower Palace Town in Seoul

Vocabulary

- **(be) jammed**: crowded
- **(be) a...life**: happens all the time, day after day, it is very normal
- **to stand idle**: be unused
- **under...crowd**: anybody who is younger than 30 years old
- **primarily...of**: mostly for the convenience of
- **every conceivable**: every fast food chain that anybody can think of
- **skyscraper**: a building 20 stories or more in height

Modern buses like this are very recent.

Public transportation before 1990 was primitive compared to what it is today. Seoul had a subway, but only a couple of lines, and buses were rickety. There were no automatic fare collecting machines inside the buses, as there are today. Instead, bus girls collected the fare (bus *boys* in Jeju) which in 1982 was about 40 won. In most cases, bus stops weren't even marked.

If you needed to buy something late at night, there was no place to buy it. There was a midnight-to-4 a.m. curfew in Korea until 1982 due to the North Korean threat, so all stores were closed. Even after the curfew was stopped, it was still hard to shop at night because there were no convenience stores.

> "Most of the things that today's young people take for granted didn't even exist in the mid-90s."

Most of the things that today's young people take for granted didn't even exist before the mid-1990s. There were no computers or Internet, so no Internet chat rooms or Internet gaming. Young people spent their time playing video arcade games like *Pac Man* and *Breakout* that are primitive by today's standards.

There were no discount stores, no credit cards and no ATM machines. When you wanted to buy a train ticket, you had to go to the station and stand in a long line. You couldn't make an online reservation because there was no Internet.

Schools were not coeducational, and the worst things that high school boys could do were to have hair longer than 3 cm. or smoke cigarettes.

Pac-Man, so primitive.

Vocabulary

- **primitive**: very inconvenient, very basic, not comfortable
- **rickety**: noisy, gives a bumpy ride
- **bus girls**: girls who collected the fare from passengers after they boarded the bus
- **bus...marked**: there was no sign showing where the bus stopped, you just had to know
- **curfew**: period of time when nobody could go outside
- **take...granted**: expect to have, cannot live without
- **online reservation**: booking made on the Internet, without going to the train station
- **coeducational**: boys and girls going to the same school

Society

WORD PRACTICE

Fill in the correct word.

1. Koreans under 40 can't____to the way Korea was in the 1980s.
2. Every TV news____began with news about Chun Du Hwan.
3. In the 1980s Korea had no modern communication____.
4. Missed appointments were a____of life.
5. Korea's first fast food restaurants were for the____of foreigners.
6. Phone booths that used to be____with people now stand____.
7. Compared to today, public transportation was____.
8. People take for____things that didn't even exist in the 1980s.
9. There was a midnight to 4 a.m.____until 1982.

a. broadcast
b. curfew
c. idle
d. relate
e. granted
f. primitive
g. jammed
h. benefit
i. way
j. devices

Answers on page 160.

DISCUSS

1. Compare Korean life before 1990 with life today in regard to each of the following. *(If you're not sure, just tell what you THINK it must have been like.)*
   a. public transportation
   b. televisions
   c. TV broadcasting (types of programs, number of channels, etc.)
   d. contacting people, keeping in touch, keeping appointments
   e. shopping for food and things
   f. car ownership, traffic, air pollution
   g. outdoor advertising and neon signs
   h. fast food restaurants
   i. popular foods
   j. quality of education
   k. paying for things, using cash

1980 TV

2. Describe what it would be like to live with a nighttime curfew, which Koreans had until 1983. Does it sound scary? How would you feel if you could not go out at night? Would that affect your lifestyle? If so, in what way?
3. Do you think that Korea's image abroad (in the eyes of foreigners) has improved much since the 1980s? If so, which physical changes or events would be most responsible for causing foreigners to change their opinion about Korea?
4. Have all the changes that Korea has undergone since 1990 been positive, or was Korea a better place to live in the 1980s? What are some of today's problems that probably didn't exist back then?
5. Middle and high school students a generation ago were better behaved than the students of today. Why do today's teenagers do more bad things? What has changed to make them do bad things?
6. Judging by the behavior of today's middle and high school students, do you think the schools of today are better or worse than the schools of the 1980s? Tell why you think so.
7. If you had a chance to visit Korea during the 1980s, would you do it? If so, what would you want to experience (do/see) the most?
8. What do you think of skyscraper condominiums? Which would you rather live in—one on the 7th floor, built in 1990, or one on the 59th floor, built in 2013?

UNIT 2

Pirated Korean Goods

Hyundai Santa Fe and Chinese copycat version.

An amazing turnaround has happened in Korea in the past twenty years concerning pirated goods. In the 1980s foreign brands and the Korean government were struggling to control the manufacture and sale of copycat products in Korea.

Just two decades later Korean-made products are now being pirated. Everything from Korean designer clothing to Korean electronics and Korean automobiles are being duplicated in China. The most shocking thing of all is that many of these products are even being sold in Korea, robbing Korean companies of their own market. It is a stunning development that no one in Korea 20 years ago could have imagined in their wildest dreams.

When China's Huanghai Motors unveiled their new SUV at the Beijing Auto Show in November of 2006, people could hardly believe their eyes. The car looked like a replica of Hyundai's 2007 Santa Fe.

The Chinese car maker had combined the designs of two different Korean cars—the Santa Fe and the Kia Sorrento—in a slick attempt to avoid being dragged into court on a piracy charge. By combining features of two cars it could not be shown in court that their product was an exact copy of any other product.

Kia Sorrento

Vocabulary

- **turnaround**: reversal of roles, the exact opposite came true
- **pirated goods**: imitations of famous brand products
- **copycat products**: exact copies of famous brand products
- **stunning**: amazing, shocking, almost unbelievable
- **could...dreams**: no one could have predicted it to happen
- **replica**: exact copy, a duplicate
- **slick**: wise but dishonest
- **dragged...charge**: be sued in a court of law

The Chinese govt. is trying to crack down on piracy.

The number of Korean products being duplicated in China is mindboggling. Chinese pirates are counterfeiting almost everything made in Korea from cell phones and electronics, household appliances to steel, auto parts, even snack foods. It is hurting Korean exports enormously and costing Korean manufacturers a huge amount of money in lost profits. The Korea International Trade Association estimated that Chinese piracy of Korean goods cost Korea 1.3 trillion won (US$15 billion) in 2006.

Some start-up Korean companies have been forced out of business because a month after they introduce a new product or design, Chinese pirates release an exact copy of their product at half the price. There is no way that Korean manufacturers can compete with products out of China, where factory wages are one-tenth of what they are in Korea.

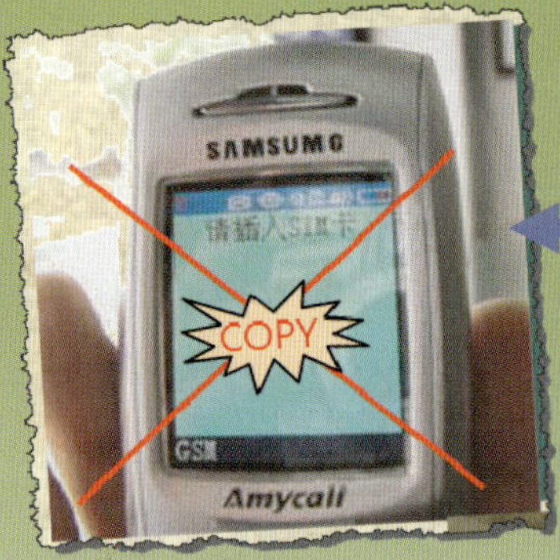

Chinese pirates imitate brand names. Change the "n" to an "m" and the Samsung Anycall becomes Samsumg Amycall.

Chinese pirates are even brazen enough to imitate logos. This "Sammeng" logo is exactly the same as the Samsung logo.

iPhones: Can u tell them apart?

Chinese pirates love to copy Korean electronics.

Vocabulary

- **mindboggling**: really amazing
- **counterfeiting**: copying, duplicating
- **enormously**: to an extreme degree
- **start-up**: new company just starting out
- **There...way**: It is impossible
- **to compete**: sell products cheaper than competitors
- **brazen**: not ashamed or embarrassed to do it

This "Sammeng" ad with the face of Korean star Song Hye-gyo

The worst part of the problem is that the quality of the products coming out of China today is in most cases almost equal to that of the Korean originals themselves. A few years ago it would have been possible to look at a Chinese counterfeit and immediately distinguish it from the real thing, but that's no longer true. Today, China is equipped with the latest cutting-edge technology which they received from Korea and Japan back in the 1990s, so their products are just about as good.

It is ironic that Korea and Japan, the two countries being hurt the most by Chinese piracy, are the ones who gave China the technology in the first place. It's a classic example of shooting oneself in the foot. Eager to take advantage of China's low factory wages, they both rushed to build factories in China during the 1990s.

They never dreamed that their scheme to become more competitive in the world marketplace would end up backfiring. Now China is using the technological expertise they got from Japan and Korea to steal their markets away from them.

Another huge irony for Korea and Japan is that Chinese counterfeit goods are sold even in their own countries. Hyundai, Kia, and Daewoo car parts made in Chinese factories are cheaper than the originals made in Korea.

Chery Motors priced their QQ minicar 30% lower than Daewoo's Matiz and **stole away** the market in Venezuela.

Vocabulary

- **to distinguish**: be able to tell them apart, which is the original and which is the fake
- **cutting edge**: most modern, newest, up to date
- **in...place**: in the first place
- **classic**: excellent, perfect
- **shooting...foot**: expression that means unintentionally doing harm to oneself
- **to backfire**: give the exact opposite result (in this case, hurt them instead of help them)
- **to steal away**: replace them as being the top seller

LOOKS the same, but NOT the same

In this crash test, the driver of the Matiz lived, but the driver of the QQ was killed.

DISCUSS

1. Did you know about this Chinese piracy problem of Korean goods before reading the article? If so, where did you hear about it?
2. How do you feel after reading this article? Tell why you feel that way.
    - Angry.
    - Shocked.
    - All companies do the same thing.
    - The Chinese are very clever.
3. What do you think of the pirates who copy Korean goods?
    - They're thieves.
    - They're good businessmen.
    - Have no creativity, no ideas of their own = not smart.
4. Do you think most people who buy the pirated goods realize they are buying copies and not the originals? Do they know the difference between Samsung and imitations like Samsumg or Samesong or do they think they are buying Korean products?
5. During a 100-day anti-piracy campaign in 2006 the Chinese government reported having seized 58 million pirated goods and sentencing piraters to life imprisonment.
    a. Do you believe it? Why or why not?
    b. Do you think life imprisonment is a fair punishment for piraters?
6. Why is it important for governments to stop piracy? What can foreign countries do to retaliate (fight back) against countries that allow piracy to continue?
7. Chinese pirates are not ashamed to make look-alike products with look-alike names. What kind of people would work in that kind of business? Same as gangsters? Uneducated? Would you do it if you knew you could make a lot of money?
8. Twenty years ago Koreans were doing the same thing that the Chinese are now doing. Is there any difference between the two cases, or are they just the same?
9. What, if anything, can be done to stop the Chinese from copying Korean products? Can Korean companies or the Korean government do anything to stop it? If so, what?
10. Why does the Korean government allow Chinese imitations of Korean products to be sold in Korea? Isn't that a little strange?
11. Chinese counterfeiters seem to love to copy Korean hi-tech products
12. How can you explain their fascination with Korean-made products?

UNIT 3

Online Sex Trade

Women renting boys for sex

In 2004 the Korean government passed an anti-prostitution law as part of its clampdown on the sex trade in order to protect teenage girls from adult sex predators.

But 3 years later Seoul police were shocked to find that they'd been worrying about the wrong age group. It wasn't adult men who were preying on the girls but the girls' own peers—teenage boys acting as pimps in an ever-widening wave of teenage prostitution to serve other teenage boys.

In some cases the pimps weren't boys but other teenage girls. One 14-year-old Koyang (Kyeonggi) girl was arrested for forcing two of her classmates to have sex with three middle school boys.

Seeing the easy money that girls were making, some of the boys decided they also wanted a piece of the action and started selling sex to "older" women in their 20s to 40s. Like the girls, the boys advertised their sexual services on the Internet.

In 2010 Korean police shut down hundreds of prostitution websites and chat rooms that introduced older women to young men and boys for sex. One website had a membership of over 550 women all wanting to have sex with young boys.

> One website had a membership of 550 older women wanting boys and young men for sex.

Prostitution has always been illegal in Korea, but it has gone on openly in "room salons" and red light districts. But the availability of sex through the Internet creates a whole new class of criminals that is almost beyond the reach of the police because the deals are made in the privacy of people's homes.

Street walkers in Europe

Vocabulary

- **clampdown**: strong move to stop it completely
- **sex trade**: prostitution, getting paid to have sex
- **adult...predators**: older men wanting young girls for sex
- **to prey (on)**: to make them victims, using them to fulfill their desires
- **pimps**: people who find customers for the prostitutes for a commission
- **easy money**: make big money doing something that isn't like work
- **a...action**: make some big money, same as the girls are doing

Society

This situation provides more fuel to the argument that Korea's rush to be the first wired nation on earth may have been a big mistake. Korea's teen hookers and hustlers are engaging in a kind of illegal eCommerce, Three out every ten Internet chatting websites in Korea are used for the prostitution of teenage girls or boys.

Half of the girls being arrested are under the age of 16, some as young as 13. The male prostitutes arrested are mostly high school or university students but also include some salaried workers in their 20s who supplement their incomes by having sex with middle-aged women.

A red-light district in Seoul

While all the young men selling sex do it voluntarily, that's not true for all of the girls. Many are doing it against their will, and they're not getting any of the money. They are being bullied and threatened by their classmates and violated by their customers. In other words, they are being raped.

In 2010 Jeju police arrested an 18-year-old boy for forcing a 15-year-old girl to have sex with 24 men in their 20s and 30s more than 75 times. He then took all of the 1.1 million won that she had earned and raped her. He's now in prison.

Arrested in Jeju for forcing one girl to service 24 older men regularly.

Vocabulary

- **fuel...fire**: makes their case stronger, it seems to prove what they already said
- **hookers...hustlers**: slang words for female and male prostitutes, respectively
- **supplementing...incomes**: making some extra money, like a part-time job
- **against...will**: don't want to do it
- **(be) bullied**: forced to do things they don't want to do
- **(be) violated**: be attacked physically
- **(be) raped**: to have sex forced on them

A Phnom Pehn, Cambodia brothel

Koreans' use of the Internet to find sex extends outside Korea. With so many Koreans now traveling or working in S.E. Asia, sex businesses there are now catering to Korean men. They advertise their services on Korean online community websites.

Rent-a-hooker online service

Book sex before leaving home.

A government investigation in 2010 found one tourist agency posting sex tour schedules and information about their prostitutes and even their prices, ranging from 1.2 to 2.2 million won. Another website was recruiting Korean women to work as prostitutes in their brothel.

Of three Phnom Pehn, Cambodia brothels that were checked out said they catered to Korean male tourists in particular. One of those places hired underage girls, inferring that some Korean men were travelling to SE Asia to buy sex with young girls.

The Cambodian government has been trying to eradicate the teenage sex trade in their country, and distributes pamphlets about their campaign, printed in just 3 languages: Khmer (Cambodian), English, and Korean.

Many Koreans worry about the damage this situation is doing to the Korean image abroad. They complain that the Korean government should be doing something to halt the Korean men from traveling abroad in order to buy sex. They think that the government should at least shut down the websites of businesses that advertise sex travel and prostitution abroad.

In 2008 the Korean government has been revoking passports of men caught buying sex abroad, but very few of the men who return from sex tours are ever arrested.

Vocabulary

- **to cater to**: direct their service to a particular person or group
- **online...websites**: chatrooms and online discussion forums
- **to recruit**: try to hire, want to hire them
- **brothel**: house of prostitution, where girls are available for sex
- **underage**: younger than 18 years old
- **Korean...abroad**: what people in foreign countries think of Koreans
- **to halt**: make it stop, discontinue
- **to revoke**: take away from them, make it no longer usable

A Cambodian brothel

WORD PRACTICE

Fill in the correct word.

1. In 2004 the government decided to____on the online sex trade.
2. Teenage boys were____on the girls, acting as____.
3. Boys wanted to make some of that____money too.
4. Korea's rush to become a____country may have been a mistake.
5. The present situation adds more____to that argument.
6. Many brothels in SE Asia now____to Korean men.
7. Some websites____Korean women to work in____.
8. The Korean government____passports of men buying sex abroad.

a. preying
b. fuel
c. wired
d. brothels
e. clampdown
f. recruit
g. revokes
h. pimps
i. cater
j. easy

Answers on page 160.

DISCUSS

1. How serious is the teen prostitution problem for the society? Tell why you think so.
   a. It is very serious for the country.
   b. It isn't serious because it's normal for teenagers to want to have sex.
2. Which of these problems is worse? Tell why you think so.
   a. Older men having sex with teenage girls is worse.
   b. Older women having sex with young boys is worse.
   c. They're both the same—very bad.
3. What do you think about the government arresting men who buy sex abroad?.
   a. Good idea. They deserve to be arrested.
   b. Bad idea. Men should be allowed to go on sex tours if they want to.
4. Who or what is to blame for Korea's teenage sex trade? Give a percentage to each, then tell why you think so.
   - ___% The Internet chat rooms
   - ___% Parents
   - ___% Schools
   - ___% Korean society

Internet porn site

5. How should each of the participants in the sex trade be punished?
   - Pimps (boys or girls) who find the customers and then take the money
   - The boy and girl prostitutes (who do it to make money)
   - The prostitutes' customers (teenagers or adults)
6. Is there any way to stop the teenage sex trade in Korea? How can the police stop the pimps, prostitutes, and customers?
7. Since 95% of the teenage prostitution is done on adult dating chat rooms, should those websites be banned? Why or why not?
8. Which of these statements do you agree with? Tell why.
   - Giving teenagers information about sex and will make them have less sex.
   - Discussing sex with teenagers will make them want to have sex even more.
9. Older men have always wanted young girls for sex, but why are Korean women now looking for younger men and teenage boys? What has changed in society to make this happen?
10. Should the Korean government try to stop men from having sex in foreign countries? Is that the government's role, or is it none of their business?

UNIT 4 Suicides in Korea

Every day 38 people commit suicide in Korea. That is more than three times more than in the USA (10) and ten times more than in Greece (3). Korea's suicide rate is 24.3 per 100,000 people, putting it first in the world in suicides, with Hungary coming in second at 21 suicides per 100,000.

Korea didn't always have such a high suicide rate. In 1982 Korea's suicide rate was just 6.8; it has increased 600% since then. Between 2003 and 2008 Korea's suicide rate increased from 18.1 to 24.3

In terms of the rate of increase of the suicide rate, Korea also ranks number one in the world. The number of suicides in Korea increases by 1% every year. Mexico is second at 0.61% and Japan, third at 0.44%.

Suicide rate in OECD member countries (per 100,000 people)

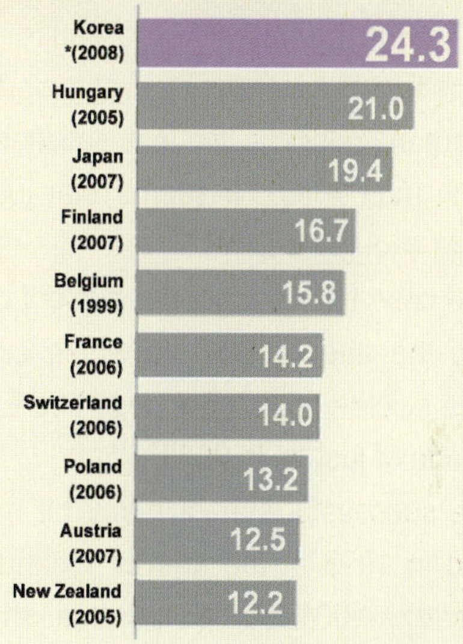

* Year data was compiled

Source : Ministry of Health & Welfare

Why are so many Koreans committing suicide? Why is it that 30 years ago when Koreans were poor by today's standards, very few people killed themselves, but now that Koreans are affluent and have all of the nicer things of life, more and more people want to die? If there ever was a perfect example of the old saying, "Money can't buy happiness", this would be it.

Vocabulary

- **to commit suicide**: kill oneself
- **rate...increase**: how fast the number of suicide cases is increasing each year
- **by...standards**: compared to the comfortable lives Koreans have today
- **affluent**: rich, wealthy
- **all...life**: nice home, nice car, nice clothes, etc
- **Money...happiness**: Having a lot of money doesn't guarantee that you'll be happy

Society

Suicide victim Lee Eun Ju

The rapidly rising suicide rate in Korea has had experts scratching their heads trying to figure out the cause for it. It seems that the more of life's conveniences that Koreans possess, the less satisfied they are with their lives. It seems that just the opposite should be true.

One case that brought the subject of suicide to the attention of the whole country was the suicide death of actress Lee Eun Ju at the age of just 24 in 2005.

The successful star of many hit movies starting in 1998 at the age of 18 and later the star of a 2004 television drama, she had everything to live for, or so it seemed. But just days after she graduated from college her brother found her hanging with her wrists slashed in her bedroom closet.

Notes left behind by the star provided some clues as to the possible cause of many of the suicides taking place today: social pressure. In Ms. Lee's case, it was pressure from Korean society as to how women should behave. In her final film she played the part of a man's mistress, and there were many sex scenes in that film. Because of that, she had severe insomnia, worrying about what the role was doing to her reputation.

She should have sought counseling for her problem but didn't do so because Koreans are suspicious of people who seek the advice of psychiatrists. Most Koreans assume that anyone who goes to a mental health professional must be crazy.

A hanging suicide victim.

"Most Koreans assume that anyone who goes to a mental health professional must be crazy."

Vocabulary

- **scratching...heads**: trying to figure it out, find an answer
- **life's conveniences**: things that make life comfortable, like a car
- **just...true**: It should make people happy, not sad.
- **wrists slashed**: she made cuts in her wrists with a knife or a razor
- **mistress**: a married man's secret sex partner
- **counseling**: getting advice from a mental health expert

- **insomnia**: inability to fall asleep

Social pressure is the reason most often given for suicides. But if Ms. Lee was worried about Koreans thinking that she was a loose woman, wasn't Korean thinking just as strict in 1982? But there were very few suicides in 1982. Why?

What's different about today and 1982 is that in 1982 there were no sex scenes in Korean films or TV dramas, so the situation that Ms. Lee faced could never happen. In those days actors weren't even allowed to kiss on screen.

Banned in the 1980s

What we have today is a liberated media but a still very conservative way of thinking that hasn't changed from a generation ago. It is a recipe for disaster.

> "What we have today...is a recipe for disaster."

Korea in the 21st century is a classic example of modernization clashing with traditional values, causing a breakdown in the social order. Studies conducted in the 1800s during the industrialization of Europe showed that as countries industrialized and urbanized, their suicide rates went up. This would explain what has happened in Korea.

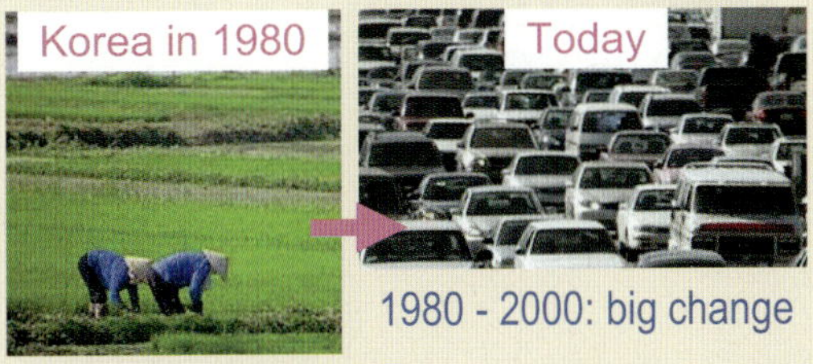

1980 - 2000: big change

Korea went from an agricultural society to an industrialized society in just 20 years. Industrialization brings problems like unemployment and the social pressure to succeed, aspects of a modernized society that are now clashing with Korea's traditional Confucist thinking.

Lowering the suicide rate will require Koreans to change their way of thinking. To prevent people from jumping to their deaths, Korean officials have tried restricting access to high buildings, but people can always find high places where they can jump from, such as from the hi-rise apartment buildings that cover Korea.

Korea's tall apartment buildings are convenient places to jump from

Vocabulary

- **loose woman**: a woman who has sex with many men
- **liberated media**: movies and TV not afraid to show sex scenes
- **recipe...disaster**: a set of conditions that is sure to cause trouble
- **to clash with**: be in conflict with, be incompatible with
- **to urbanize**: population moving from rural areas to large cities
- **Restricting...buildings**: not allowing people to go to the top of high buildings where they might jump from

Society

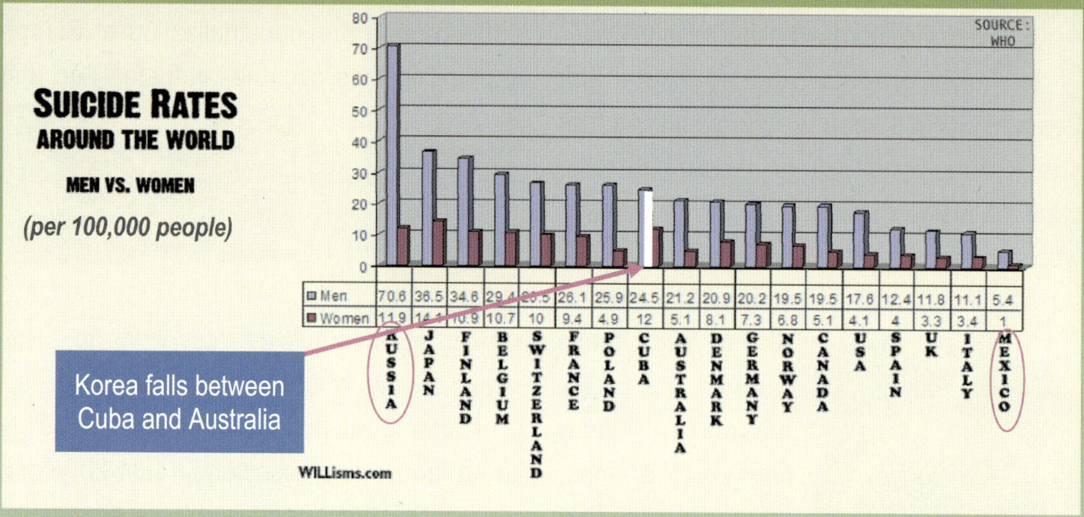

DISCUSS

1. How serious is this problem for Korea? Tell why you think so.
   - This is a very serious problem.
   - It's a serious problem for just a small percentage of people.
   - There are many problems that are more serious than this one.
2. Looking at the chart above, answer these questions:
   a. Why do you think so many more men than women kill themselves?
   b. What conclusion can you draw about life in Russia compared to life in Mexico?
3. Do you agree that the increase in Korea's suicide rate is the result of a clash between traditional Confucist thinking and modern Korean society? Does that make sense to you? Tell why you think so.
4. What's your opinion of Korean thinking in general? Which of the following statements do you agree with and why?
   - The Korean way of thinking is perfect. Everything makes sense.
   - Korean thinking is old fashioned, and that causes social problems.
5. Do you think that Korean society will ever abandon its Confucist principles and become liberal? If so, a) what will make it happen and b) how many years will it take to change? If it will never change, why not?
6. What are the factors that contribute to so many Koreans killing themselves? Consider each of the following possible factors. Name others if you can think of any.
   - Unemployment / hard job
   - Love affairs
   - Unhappy marriage or divorce
   - Don't earn enough money
7. Considering the suicide of actress Lee Eun Ju, do you agree or disagree with each of the following statements?
   a. Her suicide shows the strong pressure put on Korean women by the society.
   b. Traditional Korean thinking helped to kill her by preventing her from seeking the advice of a mental health professional.
8. If a close friend was feeling depressed would you advise him or her to seek the advice of a mental health professional or would you try to help them yourself? Do you think that people who seek professional counseling are crazy? Why or why not?

UNIT 5

The Korean Space Program

Society

If the Korea Aerospace Research Institute (KARI) has its way, South Korea will be one of the world's top 10 aerospace powers by 2015. That may come as a surprise to people who haven't been following the ambitious Korean space program, which started way back in 1987.

Korea's first experimental satellite (Kitsat 1) was successfully launched in 1992. Just three years later, in 1995, the telecommunications satellite Koreasat 1 was launched, making South Korea only the 23rd nation in the world to be operating a commercial satellite. That was quite an accomplishment for a country that was still recovering from a destructive war that had ended just 20 years earlier.

The only disappointing aspects of those early launchings were that those satellites were built in foreign countries, and the rockets propelling them into orbit were also provided by foreigners. All Korea did was to pay for them.

The first satellite built by Koreans, with the cooperation of a US firm, was the Arirang I, launched in 1999. Later, Arirang II, equipped with a high-resolution camera gave South Korea its own satellite coverage. It was built by KARI with the help of an Israeli company and cost 200 billion won.

In 2005 KARI launched the Kompsat-5 project (Korea Multi-Purpose Satellite 5) that was put into orbit in 2010. The satellite's mission is to monitor ocean, land, and weather conditions over the Korean peninsula, as well as natural disasters when they occur.

Kompsat-5

Vocabulary

- **has...way**: reaches its goal
- **aerospace powers**: countries that can send machines or men into space
- **ambitious**: having big dreams, big plans
- **launched**: began, started out
- **telecommunications satellite**: to provide satellite TV and Internet services
- **commercial satellite**: owned by private companies for the purpose of making money
- **propelling...orbit**: sending them into space, circling around the earth
- **high-...camera**: having the ability to show small details even from very far away

Society

KARI's Doheung Launch Center

When it was launched the Arirang II became Korea's seventh orbiting satellite and put South Korea in 20th place worldwide in aerospace and a producer and operators of satellites. However, launchings are still being made from foreign countries.

The reason why KARI continued using foreign-built booster rockets instead of building their own was to bypass that extremely expensive stage of development. The money saved by not building boosters could be spent on building launch pads and a launch center in Korea. Launch sites were then built at Goheung, Cholla-namdo, and Anheung in Chungchong-namdo.

KARI's launch facility at Doheung went into operation in 2006. It is a *Doppler* radar weather station, which is the latest state of the art weather prediction technology. By bouncing radio waves off objects such as clouds and raindrops, weather forecasting is more accurate than it has ever been.

Thanks to its space program Korea is now one of the few nations on earth taking advantage of this new space-age technology.

Doppler radar

Launch pad

Booster rockets

Vocabulary

- **booster rockets**: the rockets that carry the satellites into space then fall off
- **launch pads**: places where rockets carrying satellites are sent up from
- **went...operation**: began to operate, to function
- **state...art**: the latest, most recent to become available
- **Thanks to**: because of
- **taking...of**: to utilize the benefits of

The Naro Space Center, located on Oenaro Island in Cholla-namdo.

Korea took a giant leap into space with the opening of its Naro Space Center, located on Oenaro Island in Cholla-namdo, in 2008. It cost an enormous amount of money to build—265 billion won (US$285 million), but even more money was spent to launch Korean satellites from launch sites in foreign countries.

Building its own space center with launch platform was also an essential first step to take if Korea was ever to reach its goal of becoming one of the world's aerospace powers. With the opening of Naro, Korea became only the 13th country in the world to have a launch pad.

Korea has very ambitious plans for its space program, but Korean weather poses a major challenge. Liftoffs and landings can only be made in clement weather. Unfortunately, Korea is better known for its overcast skies than for cloudless blue skies like in the photos shown below.

A NASA liftoff in the USA. Korea hopes to do the same by 2015, but will the weather cooperate?

Society

Korea prepares Naro 1 for liftoff

Vocabulary

- **poses...challenge**: will be a big problem
- **liftoffs**: airplanes take off, rockets lift off
- **clement weather**: clear and sunny
- **overcast**: be covered with clouds

WORD PRACTICE

Fill in the correct word.

1. If I has its____Korea will soon be an____power.
2. Some people think the Korean space program is too____.
3. Korea is one of the few countries that has a commercial____.
4. Arirang I is equipped with a high-____camera on board.
5. At first KARI used foreign-made____rockets to save money.
6. Korea is able to take____of space age technology.
7. Korean weather____a major challenge to its space program.
8. ____and landings can only be made in____weather.

a. satellite
b. ambitious
c. advantage
d. booster
e. liftoffs
f. aerospace
g. clement
h. poses
i. way
j. resolution

Answers on page 160.

Society

DISCUSS

1. What do you think of Korea's space program? Tell why you think so.
   - I think it's great. Korea really needs a space program.
   - Korea doesn't need a space program. It's a waste of money.
2. Some people think the building of a space program in Korea is too expensive and that the money should be used on other, more important problems. Do you agree? Why or why not?
3. What do you think are the main reasons why KARI (Korea Aerospace Research Institute) wants to be one of the world's top 10 aerospace powers? Consider each of the following possible reasons. Tell why you agree or disagree.
   - ...for the worldwide prestige (fame) that will go along with being in the top 10
   - ...to give South Korea a big advantage over North Korea
   - ...to prove that Koreans are just as smart as the Japanese
   - ...to make money (build, sell and launch satellites for other countries)
4. How important is it for mankind to explore space? Is it important? Is it worth all the money that it costs? Tell why you think so.
5. What goal should Korea's aerospace industry set for itself? Tell why you think so.
   - Just the ability to build and launch communications satellites for use in Korea
   - To produce and sell satellites to other countries
   - To explore outer space, just like the US and Russia

Korea Launch Vehicle

6. If the US, Europe, and Russia are already exploring space, isn't it unnecessary and a waste of money for other countries to send up their own spaceships too? Why or why not?
7. Rocket launchings and landings require warm temperatures and clear skies. Is it reasonable to believe that Korea will ever be able to launch and land spaceships regularly, considering its cloudy, rainy or snowy winter weather? Tell why you think so.
8. Rank each of the following social issues from 1 to 6 in terms of importance to the nation. Where should Korea's money be spent? Tell why you think so.
   - Improving the educational system
   - Fighting poverty, helping poor people
   - Building roads, fighting the traffic problem
   - Building an aerospace industry
   - Looking for clean sources of energy
   - Fighting social problems like suicide

UNIT 6

Multi-Racial Korea?

It is an unfortunate fact of life in Korea, but bi-racial Koreans are second class citizens. They are victims of discrimination and social prejudice on a daily basis. The fact that they were born and raised in Korea, went to Korean schools, and speak Korean the same as everybody else carries no weight with the rest of the population. All that matters is how they look. As far as other Koreans are concerned, bi-racials are foreigners.

Koreans of mixed blood have a hard time making friends, finding jobs, and just being accepted by their neighbors. A 2002 survey found that 30 percent of bi-racial children in Korea dropped out of school because they are ignored by their classmates and treated differently by their teachers.

While there is never any excuse for discriminating against people for things they cannot help, the situation can be explained by the fact that Koreans have always been able to trace their roots back for thousands of years. Unlike multicultural western countries like the US, Canada, or Australia, Koreans have been a pure race of people for millennia.

But Koreans may be in for a big surprise because what has been true for thousands of years is changing. If the current marriage trend continues Korea will also be a multiracial society before long. il the 3 years from 2009 to 2011, 97,297 Korean men brought home foreign wives. That spells big changes for Korean demographics.

> Between 2009 and 2011, 97,297 Korean men took foreign wives.

Vocabulary

- **discrimination**: treating some people less kindly than other people
- **prejudice**: disliking someone because they are different
- **carries...weight**: doesn't matter, isn't important
- **things...help**: things they cannot change, have no control over, no responsibility for
- **millennia**: thousands of years *(plural of **millennium**, 1,000 years)*
- **be in for**: will experience
- **demographics**: the racial mix of the population

Society

Korean-Vietnamese wedding

The number of interracial marriages in Korea jumped from 4% in 2000 to 13% in 2010. 4 out of every 10 men living in rural areas are now marrying women from outside of Korea, most of them from other Asian countries. If this trend continues, then by 2020 40% of the children attending schools in rural areas will be of mixed blood. As impossible or as shocking as that may sound to Koreans, it is a fact of life they will have to get used to.

The fact that Korean men are marrying foreign women comes as no surprise. This scenario, whereby Korean men can't find women to marry, was predicted in the 1980s. Korea's traditional preference for males combined with the popularity of ultrasound to detect the sex of fetuses was resulting in female fetuses being aborted. Now children born in the 1980s are at marriageable age, and there aren't enough young women to go around.

Since they can't find wives in Korea, Korean men are forced to look for wives outside of Korea. Most of them are going to Vietnam, where women are lining up for the chance to marry Korean men. 40,000 Korean men took Vietnamese brides between 2004 and 2009.

But there is a dark side to the story as Korean men, particularly older men, are increasingly accused of beating their Vietnamese wives. So the Vietnamese government has banned its young women from marrying any Korean man aged 50 or older.

Demonstration calling attention to abuse against Vietnamese wives by their Korean husbands.

Vocabulary

- **interracial marriage**: when two people from two different races get married
- **mixed blood**: people whose parents are from two different races
- **get used to**: become adjusted to
- **scenario**: possible situation
- **ultra-...fetuses**: find out if the unborn baby is a girl or a boy using sound technology
- **(be) aborted**: be killed before it is born
- **enough...around**: not have one for each person
- **lining up**: waiting, wanting (to do something)

Some people are predicting that Korean society will split into two distinct social classes—a wealthier ruling class composed of pure-blood Koreans, and a poor, growing minority of multiracial citizens who will receive an inferior education, lower paying jobs, and fewer governmental benefits and services.

Unless Korean society makes a sudden turnaround in their acceptance of people who are different from themselves, that's what is likely to happen.

Even pure-blood Koreans who grew up abroad are not fully accepted by Korean society

In an attempt to head off potential problems for Korean society, the Korean government in 2006 came up with plans to set the country on a path toward more acceptance of multiracialism and multiculturalism. President Roh suggested a set of laws that would make discrimination of biracial citizens illegal.

Laws can be passed making discrimination illegal, but deep-seated prejudice cannot be eliminated through laws. Racism explains why biracial Koreans who don't look any different can survive at school but still don't mingle very much with classmates. That's because they feel the stigma that the society places on people who are different.

One of the laws allowed biracial Korean males to serve in the military in hopes that they would become more integrated into the society. But the law only said that they "may" serve. It didn't say that they *must* serve.

In 2009 the National Assembly changed the law, saying that it discriminated against both biracial and "Korean nationals".

But that term itself can be considered to be racist because it suggests that only people who have two Korean parents can be considered as real Korean citizens. To the average Korean, one Korean parent is not enough to make a person Korean.

A Vietnamese-American. Korea will soon be home to many Vietnamese-Koreans.

Vocabulary

- **to split**: to divide up into two parts
- **sudden turnaround**: completely change their minds about
- **to head off**: to prevent (something) from happening
- **to come...with**: to invent, devise, think about
- **racism**: disliking people just because of their race, but for no other reason
- **to mingle**: to mix with, become friends with
- **stigma**: negative public perception, making them feel ashamed
- **(be) integrated (into)**: become a part of, be fully accepted by the group

WORD PRACTICE

Fill in the correct word.

1. Bi-racial Koreans are victims of____on a daily basis.
2. Many drop out of school because they are____by classmates.
3. The fact that they speak Korean fluently____no weight.
4. Koreans have been a pure ____ for____.
5. But they may be____for a big surprise.
6. The country is rapidly becoming____.
7. Many female fetuses were____during the 1980s.
8. There is a____on being different in Korean society.
9. It is predicted that Korean society will____into two social classes.

a. millennia
b. shunned
c. multi-racial
d. race
e. discrimination
f. stigma
g. split
h. in
i. aborted
j. carries

Answers on page 160.

DISCUSS

1. Do you agree that Koreans have an underlying prejudice toward people who are different from they are? If so, why, and how did it all begin? How far back in history does it go, and can it ever change? Why or why not?
2. Do you think that the Vietnamese government is justified on banning young Vietnamese women from marrying Korean men 16 years older than they are? Who do so many Korean men beat their Vietnamese wives?
3. What is your reaction to the news that almost 100,000 Korean men married foreign women in just 3 years from 2009 to 2011? Tell why you think so.
   a. It's not good. It should be stopped.
   b. I think it's great. I would like to see Korea become multiracial like the US.
4. Do you think the current trend for Korean men to marry foreign women is just a fad that will eventually fade or will it continue?
5. If you think it will stop, what will make it stop? If you think it will continue, how will it change Korean society?

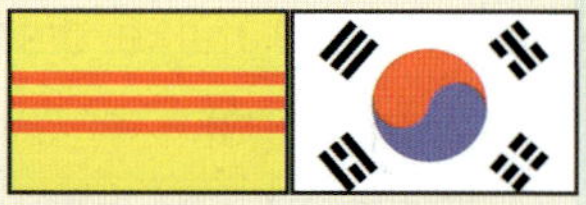

6. So many Korean men marrying Vietnamese women will create a large class of Vietnamese-Koreans, who as Korean citizens could someday be in leadership positions. Would that be okay? Why or why not?
7. Koreans criticize the Japanese for treating people with Korean ancestry who live in their country as second-class citizens. Don't Koreans do the same thing to biracials in korea? What will they do if there is a large number of biracials in Korea?
   a. They'll do the same as the Japanese—never accept biracials as real Koreans.
   b. They'll treat them the same as pure Koreans.
   c. At first there will be prejudice against them, but later they'll be accepted as Koreans.
8. What do you think about the new laws that make discrimination against biracials illegal? Will they make a difference, or will Koreans still treat biracials badly?
9. The Korean government wants to make it more difficult for Korean men to marry foreign women. Do you think that's a good idea? Why or why not?
10. Did it make any sense to give biracial Korean males the option of serving in the military while full-blooded Korean males <u>must</u> serve? What do you think?
    a. Making it an option reinforced the idea that they are different. It was a bad idea.
    b. Since only one of their parents is Korean, they shouldn't have to serve if they don't want to.

Society

UNIT 7 Military Heritage

At no time since the beginning of the Japanese occupation in 1910 has Korea been free of the sight of soldiers, military vehicles and vehicle checkpoints in various locations throughout its territory. Even after the Japanese were long gone, because of the threat of war with the North, the military continued to play a central role in Korean life.

The military governments of Park Chung Hee, Chun Doo Hwan, and Roh Tae Woo that led Korea from the end of the Korean War in 1953 until the election of Korea's first civilian president, Kim Young Sam, in 1992, used the threat of war as a means of maintaining their grip on the government and over Korean society.

Military rule finally ended with Kim's election, but even then, the military presence continued. In Korea, the sight of soldiers still is a very common sight.

A century of military rule, a military threat from the North, and the centuries-old Confucist tradition of respect for one's superiors has shaped Korean society. The military influence is visible everywhere, from company and school uniforms to the military-style discipline in schools to the way companies treat their employees.

Kim Young Sam, first civilian president

Vocabulary

- **vehicle checkpoints**: when cars are stopped and searched
- **(be) long gone**: many years after they left
- **means**: way, method
- **maintaining...grip (on)**: continue to control
- **military presence**: visibility in daily life, can be seen in public
- **respect...superiors**: willingness to obey people in higher positions
- **shaped**: formed, influenced
- **discipline**: type of punishment used, way to make them obey

Society

Japanese military-style uniform worn in Korea until the 1980s

Even with its governing role gone, the military was a part of Korean society for so long that the Korean lifestyle has taken on military characteristics of its own. Uniforms are still an important part of Korean life, and formal ceremonies are very stiff with everybody seeming to be standing at attention. High school graduations and company induction ceremonies are good examples of that.

> "People in positions of power ...are treated like generals."

To some extent Korean businesses are still run like military institutions. Employers treat their workers like soldiers who they can order around at will. Transfers to branch offices arrive like military orders, sometimes on very short notice. It is not unheard of for an employee to receive a notice on Thursday to report for work at another branch office in a city on the other side of the country the following Monday. Government employees are treated the same way.

When a company president enters the room everyone is expected to jump to his or her feet, the same way that soldiers come to attention when the company commander appears.

Meetings are formal with employees listening while the CEO or other top leaders do all of the talking. Sometimes CEOs sit on special chairs that resemble thrones.

People in positions of power, invariably men, are treated like generals. Huge offices, sometimes entire houses, are built for CEOs who may use them only a few days a year. Luxury cars and drivers are maintained for their exclusive use. To westerners, it seems that they are treated like kings.

A typical CEO car

Vocabulary

- **governing...gone**: no longer running the government
- **stiff**: rigid, not loose, not informal or relaxed
- **company...ceremonies**: welcoming a new group of employees into the company
- **at will**: as they wish, whenever they want
- **not...of**: not impossible, just the opposite
- **thrones**: the kind of seats that kings and queens sit on
- **invariably men**: always a male, never a female
- **their...use**: no one else besides the CEO may use that car and driver

None of these things seem odd to Koreans because it defines their way of life, and they have never known anything different. But to foreign visitors, particularly those from western countries, the military aspect of Korean life is very apparent.

> "Employees usually do more talking than the CEOs, the reverse of what happens in Korea."

The sight of soldiers patrolling airports or the streets would set off alarm bells in western countries. Soldiers patrolling such places symbolize trouble, a sign of war.

In western society bosses and employees are seen more as team members, everyone on the same level. Meetings are a time for employees to express their opinions and ideas while the CEOs listen and take notes. Employees usually do more talking than the CEOs do, the reverse of what happens in Korea.

The greatest influence on Korea's thinking and way of life has come from Confucianism, but the traditions of Confucianism are a model of military-style hierarchy. Dominant superiors are at the top, and they give orders to those in subservient positions. Absolute obedience is expected.

Korea has made great strides toward democracy in its political and social structures in the past two decades, but the remnants of its military past may take a long time to fade away.

Confucianism still influences Korean society heavily.

Vocabulary

- **(be) apparent**: very noticeable, quickly noticed
- **set...bells**: makes them think something is wrong
- **symbolize**: is a sign of
- **hierarchy**: system of power and responsibility
- **subservient positions**: people who have less power, those who must obey
- **absolute obedience**: must obey without asking any questions
- **strides**: progress, improvement
- **remnants**: parts left over from what was before

Society

WORD PRACTICE

Fill in the correct word.

1. There are vehicle____at various locations throughout Korea.
2. Military dictators used the____of war to hold a____on the people.
3. Uniforms reveal the military-style____present in Korean society.
4. Korean CEOs usually sit on chairs that resemble a king's____.
5. Luxury cars are maintained for their____use.
6. Employers feel they can order their employees around at____.
7. In many countries the sight of soldiers on patrol is cause for____.
8. Soldiers____trouble, a sign of war.
9. The____of its military past may take many years to erase.

a. threat
b. throne
c. discipline
d. alarm
e. grip
f. remnants
g. exclusive
h. symbolize
i. will
j. checkpoints

Answers on page 160.

DISCUSS

1. Considering the dangerous situation with the North, do you think Korea's military dictators were right to keep control of the government until 1992? Could Korea have been just as safe with a civilian government in power? Why or why not?
2. Uniforms are a part of everyday life in Korea. We can see them in banks, department stores, schools, factories, even on taxi drivers. Is the wearing of uniforms a part of Korean history or the result of the 35-years of Japanese rule?
3. What's your personal opinion about uniforms? Do you like to wear a uniform, or do you prefer wearing regular street clothes instead? Tell why you think so.
4. What do you think of the special treatment that is given to company executives—things such as big expensive cars, luxurious offices, their own personal drivers who spend most of their time sitting around doing nothing? Which of the following statements do you agree with?
   a. They deserve the special treatment because they're more important than the other workers in the company.
   b. It's a waste of the company's money.
5. Would you like to see Korea's presidents or CEOs having meetings with others at a round table, where nobody is at the head of the table, or the same way they do it now, with the president seated separately from everybody else?
6. Which has had more influence on Korean society—the military or Confucianism? Is there any difference between the military hierarchy (order of command) and Confucianism, or are they just about the same thing?
7. What social freedoms exist today that did not exist during the recent past? Do you know anything about Korean life during the 1980s when Chun Doo Hwan and Roh Tae Woo were in power? What freedoms do Koreans enjoy today that they didn't have back then?
8. Besides the school uniforms that were worn in Korea until the 1980s, what other influences did the Japanese occupation have on Korea's lifestyle? Are there any remnants still left, or have all the Japanese influences been eliminated by now?

9. People in most western countries dislike military involvement in their governments, but Asians endure it. Why are Asians less bothered by military presence than westerners?
10. Is a country with a strong military role in government safer than a country where the military plays no role? Tell why you think so.

UNIT 8

The Population Crisis

Society

The statistics are stunning: South Korea has the lowest birthrate in the world, and it's far below the minimum level needed to sustain the population. As the UK's BBC has described it, Korea's birth rate "has fallen through the floor". If it were not for the fact that Koreans are living longer, the country would already be experiencing a decline in population.

The minimum birthrate required to sustain a population is an average of 2.1 children per woman. That amounts to one child per parent, plus just a little more to compensate for the number of people dying. But in 2013 Korea's birthrate was just 1.24 children per woman, which is one child per two parents.

Due to huge improvements in health care and the standard of living, Koreans are now living longer and the population is still growing by about 1% a year. But this population increase is only because people are living longer, and people can only live for so long.

> "...by the year 2040 Korea's population will be shrinking by 1% a year."

If something isn't done to raise Korea's birthrate from what it is now Korea's population will start to decline beginning around 2020. The United Nations predicts that by the year 2040 Korea's population will be shrinking by 1% a year.

Large Korean families are a thing of the past.

Vocabulary

- **stunning**: amazing, shocking
- **to sustain**: to make it stay the same, at the same level
- **to compensate (for)**: make up for, replace
- **1.24 children**: calculated by dividing the number of babies born by the number of women of child-bearing age.
- **can...long**: people cannot live forever
- **to shrink**: become smaller

Society

The combination of a graying population with a low birthrate has an adverse effect on employment opportunities for young people. Today there are more job opportunities for people in their 40s and 50s than for young people in their 20s and 30s. This is a huge problem for college graduates, who can't find jobs, especially when business is bad.

Faced with falling profits, employers prefer to hire older, experienced workers than spend money on training new recruits fresh out of college. While that's good news for workers over 40 with families to support, the situation could be a train wreck waiting to happen for the society as a whole.

A graying population also means a coming increase in the number of retirees. It is the responsibility of the young to take care of the elderly after they leave the workforce, but a population of unemployed young people signals trouble ahead.

What makes the problem even worse is that today's college grads are very picky about the kinds of jobs they are willing to take.

Picky about jobs.

Everybody wants to work for a big company, and nobody wants to work for small or medium-sized businesses. As a result, most of them prefer to be unemployed rather than work for a company that they consider beneath their dignity.

Korea has one of the fastest aging populations in the world.

Vocabulary

- **an...effect**: cause a problem
- **when...bad**: during business slowdowns, when their profits are low
- **recruits...college**: recent college graduates
- **a...happen**: a possible disaster that may occur
- **society...whole**: the entire society
- **(be) picky**: will only accept certain [kinds of jobs], will refuse all others
- **beneath...dignity**: think they are too good to do that kind of (low-level) job

Well aware of the looming crisis, the Korean government has been scrambling to come up with ways to prevent Korea's population from going into a nosedive. One of the measures is to encourage military families to have more kids.

In 2006 the Korean Army announced that it would give special benefits to military officers, including NCO officers, and military workers who had a third child. Families with 3 children have become very rare in Korea. Under the program, the officers can choose where they want to be stationed in order to provide a stable environment for their families.

Having kids is not popular in Korea.

Beyond that, there isn't much anybody can do if Koreans don't want to have kids. It might just be that the only way Korea will be able to prevent its population from declining would be to permit immigration, the same way that multiracial western cultures like the US, Canada, and Australia do. This may seem to Koreans like a radical idea, but unless Korean couples start having more babies, there's no other way to prevent Korea from turning into a "ghost country"—a country with no people in it.

There has been some speculation as to why Koreans are having 75% fewer kids today than they did when they were poor 30 years ago. One reason could be that after being poor for so long, Koreans now just want to live the good life—have a nice house, nice car, travel, etc. The cost of educating a child has gone through the roof, leaving a family on a modest income with almost no money to spend on entertainment, nice clothes, cars, or foreign travel.

If you can afford this car, you probably don't have any kids.

Vocabulary

- **looming crisis**: crisis about to occur
- **to scramble**: to struggle eagerly, with great difficulty
- **go...nosedive**: to fall suddenly and very fast
- **measures**: ways, methods
- **to be stationed**: to be located (used only with military personnel)
- **speculation**: guessing, suggesting
- **live...life**: have many nice things and lots of money to spend

WORD PRACTICE

Fill in the correct word.

1. Korea's birthrate is too low to____the current population level.
2. Korea's population will start to____in 2040.
3. People living longer has an____effect on youth employment.
4. Companies don't want to spend the money to train new____.
5. That could be a train____waiting to happen.
6. College grads are very____about the jobs they'll do.
7. The Korean government is aware of the coming____.
8. There has been some____as to why Koreans aren't having kids.
9. Today's Koreans would rather____the good____than have kids.

a. shrink
b. recruits
c. speculation
d. picky
e. adverse
f. life
g. crisis
h. wreck
i. live
j. sustain

Answers on page 160.

DISCUSS

1. Do you agree that it is important for Korea to sustain or increase its population? Why or why not?
2. What are some of the problems that could occur if Korea's population starts to fall? How would it affect the following?
   - Korea's ability to maintain an effective military force
   - Korea's ability to remain as one of the world's economic powerhouses
   - Korea's ability to take care of its old people
   - The employment situation gets even worse
3. What do you think of the government's plan to encourage military families to have more children? Is it a good idea? Do you think it will work? Why or why not?
4. Can the Korean government solve the population crisis? Which do you agree with?
   - The government should encourage people to have more children.
   - It's a private matter, and the government should not be telling people how many children to have.
5. Are there any advantages that could come from having a smaller population? If so, what would they be?
6. Besides encouraging military families to have more children, is there anything the government could do to encourage other Koreans to have more kids? If so, what?
7. It is suggested that the reason Korean couples are having fewer children now than when they were poor is today's high cost of education, including after-school hagwon classes. Do you agree that the cost of education could be responsible for families deciding to have fewer children?
8. If you agree that the cost of educating a child in Korea is preventing children from being born, isn't it time to ban hagwon classes? Why or why not?
9. Can hagwons be forced to lower their prices so that more students can afford to go?
10. What do you think is a suitable number of children to have? Would you consider having three or four children? Why or why not?
11. What do you think of allowing foreigners to immigrate into Korea, the same as the US and Canada do? Wouldn't that solve the population problem? Why or why not?

Korean Air is busier now.

UNIT 9

Racism in Korea

A rare sight in Korea

One thing about Korea that foreigners know more about than even Koreans themselves is the degree of racism that exists in the country. It's something that Koreans don't really think about, never talk about, and may not even be aware of, but racism does indeed exist in Korea. Ask any non-white foreigner who has ever tried to get a job teaching English here.

When it comes to getting a job teaching English in a Korean hagwon, appearance usually takes precedence over educational background and teaching credentials.

As ludicrous as it may be, whites who learned English as a second language have been known to get jobs teaching English while well-qualified non-white native speakers were turned away.

> "Appearance usually takes precedence over educational background and teaching credentials."

One disgruntled native speaker disgusted with the hiring practices at the hagwon where he was working filed a complaint with the Ministry of Education.

He reported watching applications from people with excellent teaching qualifications being thrown into the trash before a young woman with bleached blond hair but no college degree and no teaching experience was picked for the job.

Having blond hair qualifies you to teach English.

Vocabulary

- **racism**: disliking people for no other reason than their race
- **takes...over**: is considered to be more important than...
- **teaching credentials**: past teaching experience, qualifications for the job
- **ludicrous**: nonsense, ridiculous, foolish
- **(be) turned away**: be rejected, turned down, not considered for the job
- **disgruntled**: very unhappy and complaining
- **bleached**: dyed the color blond, but original hair color was dark

Society

The racist attitude of Koreans towards non whites puts hagwon owners on the spot when it comes to the hiring of English teachers. They are, after all, businesspeople, and so they have to satisfy their students.

If they hire teachers who are unacceptable to parents, they won't have any students and will have to close down their schools.

In January of 2007 a hagwon in Seoul was so impressed with the resume of an American female applicant that they asked her to send in a photo of herself.* Thinking she was getting the job, she immediately did so.

But just minutes after she sent her photo, she received another email from the school explaining that they "hired only white people". Even worse, the email went on to say that Korea was a racist country that would never change and so she should go back to America because she would never be able to find a good job in Korea anyway.

> "The [hagwon] explained that they hired only white people."

The woman was devastated. She was half Korean. She had been born, raised, and educated in the United States, her father was an American, and English was her first language. But because her mother was Korean she was labeled a non-white.

As if to try and make her feel better, the email ended by saying that in Korea "blacks have it even worse". She had come to Korea to discover her roots, but she ended up sorry she had ever set foot in the country.

This incident was first reported on the editorial page of the Korea Times in January of 2009.

Teach English, but non-whites need not apply

Vocabulary

- **puts...spot**: place them in a very difficult position
- **resume**: listing one's education, job experience, etc.
- **went...say**: continued in saying that...
- **(be) devastated**: felt horrible, really terrible
- **have...worse**: are discriminated against even more
- **to set foot**: to enter, to come [to a place]
- **need not**: don't bother (you have no chance anyway)

Why does skin color matter so much?

The fact that even people with Korean blood are discriminated against shows just how deep racism is in Korea. What makes this situation somewhat ironic is that Korea is itself on the verge of becoming multiracial.

Because so many female fetuses were aborted in the 1980s and 1990s, the shortage of females of marriageable age is now forcing many Korean men to marry foreign women. Every year, about 30,000 Korean marriages are inter-racial.

So what's going to happen a few years from now when a significant percentage of the people born and raised in the country are only half Korean? Will citizens whose mothers were not Korean be considered foreigners, even though they have Korean fathers and speak fluent Korean?

What will happen when people whose fathers were Korean but whose mothers were SE Asian want to become Korean language (kuk-o) teachers in schools? Will they not be allowed to teach Korean because they are not 100% Korean? How far will Korean racism go?

Unfortunately, Korea has a lot of company with its 'whites only' preference. The same racism exists in most neighboring countries. Newspaper ads for English teachers in Taiwan usually contain phrases like "Western-looking applicants only" and "no ABCs *(American Born Chinese)* please."

"What makes this situation so ironic is that Korea is itself on the verge of becoming multiracial."

In other words, being a native speaker is not enough; you also have to look the part. The thinking in Taiwan is that if you're white, you look like an English teacher, but if you're not white, you don't look like an English teacher is supposed to look.

A familiar sight in Korea

Society

Vocabulary

- **(be) discriminated against**: be treated poorly by other people
- **(be) on...of**: about to become...
- **fetuses...aborted**: unborn female babies killed
- **a...percentage**: a large number or percentage
- **How...go**: to what extent will it be carried out or continued
- **to have...company**: They're not alone, many other [Asian] countries feel the same way
- **to look the part**: to look like an English teacher is supposed to look.

WORD PRACTICE

Fill in the correct word.

1. Few Koreans realize the degree of____that exists in their country.
2. Physical appearance often takes____over teaching____.
3. A woman with no experience but had____blond hair got the job.
4. The hagwon was impressed with the applicant's____.
5. The woman was____when the school rejected her application.
6. She was sorry that she ever set____in the country.
7. Korea is on the____of becoming a muli-____country.
8. Korean-Americans are also____against.

a. racism
b. resume
c. credentials
d. verge
e. precedence
f. racial
g. discriminated
h. bleached
i. devastated
j. foot

Answers on page 160.

Society

DISCUSS

1. Do you agree that Koreans have prejudices against people because of their skin color? Tell why you think so.
   - I agree that Koreans treat people with white skin better than other people.
   - It isn't true. Koreans treat everybody just the same.
2. If you were going to study English at a language institute (hagwon) which one would you choose? Tell why you would choose that hagwon. Be honest.
   - ...one where you would have a teacher with blond hair
   - ...one where you would have either a westerner or Korean-American teacher
   - ...one where you might have a teacher of any race or color skin
3. Why do Asians prefer white native speakers of English to native speakers that are considered to be non-white? What's the difference? Don't all native speakers speak the same way? Is there any good reason for choosing teachers on the basis of the color of their skin?
4. Who should be blamed for the racism in language institutes—hagwon owners or the parents of students? Isn't it true that hagwon owners won't have any students if they don't please the parents?

An American English teacher

5. How many non-white English teachers have you seen at language institutes in Korea? Do you think there are many non-white English teachers in Korea? If not, why not?
6. What do you think about the hagwon that wouldn't hire the half-Korean teacher because they hire only all-whites?
   - The school did the right thing.
   - The school was wrong. They should have hired her.
   - They should have hired her temporarily to see if the number of students dropped.
7. How do you define "non-white"? For example, is a person who is 50% Asian and 50% white-American non-white...OR...does the person have to have dark skin to be considered to be non-white?
8. What's your opinion of Korean-Americans--born and raised in the USA? Do you think of them as Koreans or as Americans? Aren't they just as qualified or less qualified to teach English than any other American with European ancestry?
9. Would you say that all Asian countries are just as racist as Korea?
10. Would you be pleased if your son or daughter decided to marry a foreigner? Why or why not?

UNIT 10

Fading Work Ethic

Before the economic crisis of 1997 it was said that the only people who could make Koreans look lazy were the workaholic Japanese. Koreans had become known for their diligence, and it was that willingness to work hard that was mostly responsible for the country's rags to riches economic development between the 1970s and the 1990s.

For a while at the beginning of the '90s it really did seem like the Koreans were becoming lazy. In a poll taken in 1996 the majority of Korean workers said that they'd rather have more time off than earn more money.

Korean companies were adopting the 5-day work week because wages had risen so much that Korean goods had lost their competitiveness abroad, reducing their profits. They had no choice but to lower labor costs, and the easiest way to do that was by reducing the number of hours employees had to work.

> "For a while...it really did seem like Koreans were becoming lazy."

By the end of 1996, much to the delight of their employees, almost every large Korean company had adopted the 5-day work week. Nobody complained about having his or her Saturdays free instead of having to go to work, even if it meant getting a smaller paycheck.

Most Korean office workers would rather take a pay cut than work more hours.

Vocabulary

- **workaholic**: spending almost all one's time working, be addicted to work
- **diligence**: willingness to work hard
- **rags...development**: being transformed from a poor country into a rich one
- **(have) time off**: not have to go to work
- **lost...abroad**: Korean products became more expensive than those from other countries
- **getting...paycheck**: earning less money

The economic crisis of 1997 changed everything. The IMF deal required Korean companies to become more efficient by cutting their bloated payrolls. That meant firing workers who were not essential to the operations of the company. Suddenly everyone was worrying about being fired or laid off. Those who were lucky enough to survive the downsizing were thankful to have kept their jobs.

"...fewer people had to do the same amount of work that had been done by more people before."

Overnight, Koreans became diligent again. Not only that, but people with jobs had to work harder. That's because with payrolls cut, fewer people had to do the same amount of work that had been done by more people before. It was 1970s déjà vu all over again. Koreans were working hard again.

A generation ago almost all Koreans had hard jobs.

The new 5-day work week had two effects—helping Korean companies to streamline their operations and spoiling Korean workers into wanting to do less work and play more.

Probably most revealing of what has happened to the Korean work ethic since the last generation was a 2007 report showing that 1.03 million Korean men were out of work but not even looking for jobs.

The 1997 Asian economic crisis had a major effect on the Korean work ethic.

Vocabulary

- **IMF deal**: the International Monetary Fund loaned money to Korea on the condition that it would eliminate wasteful spending
- **bloated payrolls**: having more employees than are needed to do the work
- **not...operations**: unnecessary workers
- **downsizing**: firing employees not needed to the business
- **déjà vu**: feels like the same thing happened once before
- **to streamline**: eliminate wasteful spending
- **to spoil**: make them lazy, want to play instead of work
- **revealing**: gives a clear picture of the situation

A company picnic.

One major change that occurred in the Korean employment system was the scrapping of the age-old tradition of lifelong relationship between employer and employee. It is another thing that today's young workers can't relate to.

Going back in Korea's economic development, being hired by a company was something like marrying into a family. Workers were expected to remain loyal to the 'family members', which consisted of everybody working for the same company.

Workers wore badges or uniforms that identified them as members, and they went on outings such as family picnics during their time off. Sometimes they took trips in company buses. They not only worked together, but they played together, and they stayed with the same company for life.

> "Workers were expected to be loyal to the 'family members', which consisted of everybody working for the same company."

Today that's history. While company employees still do some of these same things—uniforms, company trips, etc.—the idea that they will be loyal and stay with the company for life is a thing of the past. Today's workers' loyalties lie wherever the opportunities are, and for their part, employers feel the same way.

The idea of an employee quitting a company and taking a job with a competitor is not only no longer shocking but has become commonplace in Korea. It's safe to say that the traditional Korean work ethic and everything that it stood for just one generation ago no longer exists.

Nowadays employees at Korean companies come and go.

Vocabulary

- **to scrap**: get rid of, stop doing it
- **to relate to**: to know something about it
- **marrying...family**: become a close member of a group of people
- **outings**: picnics, parties, trips
- **that's history**: not true anymore, it doesn't happen anymore
- **workers...are**: you accept the best job available, even if it means changing employers
- **to come and go**: change jobs (companies) often

Society

WORD PRACTICE

Fill in the correct word.

1. Korean workers used to be known for their____.
2. Korean companies adopted a 5-day____week.
3. Workers prefer to have more time____than a bigger____.
4. High wages can cause Korea to lose its____abroad.
5. The IMF deal forced companies to cut their____payrolls.
6. Companies had to____in order to survive the crisis.
7. Lifetime company loyalty is a____of the past.
8. Employees used to go on____with their colleagues and families.
9. Today's young workers can't____to how it used to be.

a. relate
b. paycheck
c. off
d. bloated
e. thing
f. downsize
g. work
h. outings
i. diligence
j. competitiveness

Society

DISCUSS

Answers on page 160.

1. Would you agree in saying that Koreans today do not work as hard as Koreans one or two generations ago? If so, what do you think explains the change? Why don't they work as hard?
2. What do you think of the 5-day work week? Tell why you think so.
   a. It's a good idea. People need to enjoy their lives.
   b. It's a bad idea. Too much free time makes people lazy.
3. How do you think Koreans rank in regard to diligence when compared to...
   - ...Japanese people? Are Koreans lazier, more diligent or about the same?
   - ...Chinese people?
   - ...people from English-speaking countries?
   - ...people in southeast Asia?
   - ...North Koreans?
4. Which system of employment is better—the traditional Korean work ethic whereby workers are part of the company for life, or the modern concept whereby workers can change companies anytime they want? Tell why you think so.
5. The economic crisis of 1997 caused big changes in the way that Korean businesses operate. Based on what you just read in the article, do you think the changes were probably good or bad for the country? Tell why you think so.
6. Do you agree or disagree that Korean workers today would rather spend more time playing than working? If true, doesn't that make them lazy? Why or why not?
7. How would you describe yourself—diligent or lazy? Are you a person who likes to work, or do you hate to work? Explain.
8. What do you think of the 5-day work week? If you could decide how many days off you could have per week, how many days would you choose—2 days off? 3 days off? More? Tell why.
9. What helps the most in making a country prosperous—a) natural resources, b) education, or c) the diligence of its citizens? Tell why you think so.
10. How do you compare with your parents in regard to diligence? Are your parents more diligent than you are? If so, does that mean you are spoiled? Why or why not?
11. Will the old style company loyalty ever return to Korean businesses, or is it gone forever?

A job for hard workers

UNIT 11 Emigration

One of many "Koreatowns" in North America

Fifty thousand Koreans crammed into COEX in September of 2006, all with one purpose in mind—getting out of Korea for one reason or another.

The event was the Korea Student and Emigration Fair, held twice a year—every March and September. What was special about this fair, besides the fact that it drew 40% more visitors than the one held in March, was that for the first time ever the focus was on Southeast Asia instead of the US, Canada, New Zealand, or Australia.

125,000 Koreans emigrated to English-speaking countries between 1995 and 2005—mostly to the US and Canada—but almost nobody moved to Southeast Asia. All of a sudden, that's now changing.

Four of the ten countries represented at the fair were SE Asian—Thailand, Malaysia, the Philippines, and Singapore. The number of agency booths for emigration to those countries increased from 10 in March to 30 in September. Another 46 booths represented schools in Southeast Asia. That was twice the number of booths of the year before.

필리핀 유일의 캐나다 어학원!

Why go far away to Canada when you can go to a Canadian school in the sunny Philippines?

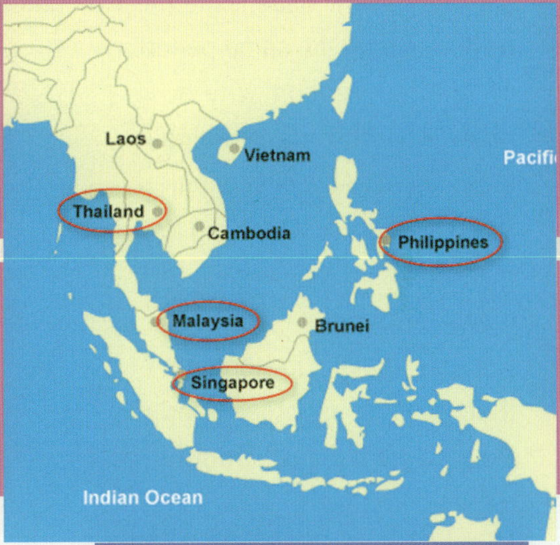

SE Asia: the new destination for Korean students and retirees.

Vocabulary

- **to cram into**: squeeze into, the implication is that there was a huge crowd of people attending the fair
- **emigration**: moving to other countries
- **to draw**: to attract, to gather
- **all...sudden**: suddenly, without warning or expectation
- **retirees**: people who stop working due to old age

Khrabi, Thailand

There are a few reasons why Koreans are suddenly interested in going to Southeast Asia. One of them is the tightening of requirements to get into western countries. Illegal aliens have become a major problem and an important social issue, especially in the US, and that has caused much tighter screening of people wanting to immigrate.

> "Retirees just can't make it in Korea on their meager incomes."

Emigration of Koreans to Canada fell by 22% between 2003 and 2004, and the number of US work visas issued to Koreans fell by 30% during the same period.

Another reason why so many Koreans are heading to Southeast Asia is economics. The high cost of living is making it hard for Koreans to make ends meet. Retirees just can't make it in Korea on their meager incomes, and they've heard that people can live better in Southeast Asia than they can in Korea on the same amount of money.

High prices in Korea also explains why Korea is being dropped from the itineraries of some foreign tourists. 5,000 people participated in an online survey taken by the Pacific Area Travel Association (PATA) in 2007 and ranked South Korea 10th among 14 Asian countries that they would most like to visit. Thailand was number one.

The main reason why Korea ranked so low on the list? Too expensive. Just one night at a small business hotel in Seoul costs more than two nights at a plush 4-star hotel on Thailand's tropical resort island, Phuket.

This plush hotel in Thailand is 50% cheaper than a tiny business hotel in Seoul.

Vocabulary

- **tightening**: making it more difficult than before
- **screening**: carefully checking on the people who are applying
- **make...meet**: have enough money to pay for all the expenses
- **can't...it**: don't make enough money to pay all of their expenses
- **meager incomes**: small amounts of money that they receive each month
- **itineraries**: travel schedules, expected stops during their travel
- **plush**: luxurious and comfortable

Koreans in their 50s and 60s in particular are leaving Korea in droves for Southeast Asia. The reason most of them give for leaving is that they can't afford to live in Korea anymore. The cost of living has gone through the roof, so their choice is either to live like paupers in Korea or go south where they can live comfortably. The number of Koreans who emigrated to either the Philippines or Vietnam doubled between 2005 and 2006. Others have settled in Malaysia and the south of Thailand.

WINTER IN SE ASIA
WINTER IN KOREA

"Most people would rather spend the winter on a beach in Southeast Asia than in Korea."

One thing that entices many Korean retirees to emigrate to Southeast Asia is the weather. It's a lot easier to stay healthy in the warm weather of Southeast Asia than in Korea's wintry weather. Cold winters cause most older people to stay cooped up inside the house for months on end. Most people would rather spend the winter on a beach in Southeast Asia than in Korea.

Something else that encourages Korean émigrés are the immigration policies of Southeast Asian countries, unlike the obstacles *against* immigration set up by the Korean government. Anyone who deposits 45 million won in a Malaysian bank can live there permanently, but the longest any non-Korean can stay in Korea without having full time employment is 3 months.

All that is required for a renewable 1-year "retirement visa" in Thailand is a document showing a foreign income of about 2.5 million won a month.

A Korean restaurant in SE Asia

Vocabulary

- **...in droves**: in large numbers
- **to go...the roof**: to become extremely expensive
- **live...paupers**: live like poor people, spend as little money as possible
- **to entice**: cause them to want to go there, to attract them
- **be cooped up**: closed in, not able to go outside
- **for...end**: for many months
- **can...permanently**: never has to leave as long as the money stays in the local bank

Society

WORD PRACTICE

Fill in the correct word.

1. So many people were____into that concert hall.
2. The fair____visitors from all over the world.
3. SE Asia looks good to____who are living on a small income.
4. People who want to immigrate receive a thorough____.
5. Korea was dropped from their____because it was too expensive.
6. High living costs makes it hard for retirees to____ends meet.
7. The harsh winters cause older people to stay____up inside....
8. ...the house for months on____.
9. SE Asia's warm weather____many Koreans to_____there.

a. retirees
b. make
c. itinerary
d. emigrate
e. crammed
f. entices
g. screening
h. end
i. drew
j. cooped

Answers on page 160.

DISCUSS

1. How does it make you feel to know that many Koreans are moving away from Korea? Tell why you think so.
   a. I'm angry. They shouldn't leave their native land.
   b. They're probably doing the right thing.
   c. I don't care if Koreans want to move out.
2. What do you think of studying English in the Philippines or Malaysia instead of the US, Canada, the UK or Australia? Can you learn English just as well? What are the advantages and disadvantages of studying English in Southeast Asia instead of in those other far away countries?
3. Do you agree that Korea has become too expensive a place to live? Compare the cost of living in Korea today with about 10 years ago. What things are more expensive today than they were back then?
4. What do you think of all the elderly Koreans now deciding to retire in Southeast Asia? Do you agree with any of these statements?
   a. They have no choice because they can't afford to live in Korea.
   b. They should stay in Korea and let their children take care of them.
   c. They probably just want to live in a warm place.
5. Would you ever consider emigrating to another country? If so, where? Would you ever consider moving to Southeast Asia? Why or why not?
6. Tourism to Korea has dropped because one night in a small hotel in Seoul costs more than two nights in a luxury hotel in Southeast Asia. Should Korean hotels lower their prices? Is that even possible? What's the best way to make tourists want to take vacations in Korea?
7. Would you like to see Korea have the same kind of liberal immigration policies that Southeast Asian countries have, that allow people to live there just by having some money in a local bank? Why or why not?

8. Why does Korea have strict immigration policies while SE Asian countries have liberal policies? Tell why you think so.
9. Where do you think is a better place to live—in a warm climate or one that has cold winters? Why?
10. Where would you rather spend the winter—in Korea or in SE Asia? Why?

UNIT 12 The Korean Wave

Korean Wave: How long can it last?

When the words "Korean exports" are uttered, the things that usually come to mind are state of the art automobiles, flat screen TVs, and everything else high tech.

The foreign money taken in from the sale of these products abroad is considerable, but they are not the only Korean exports infusing the Korean economy with foreign cash. It's called *K-pop*, short for *Korean Pop*, also known as the *Korean Wave*, and its contribution to the Korean economy each year is a staggering 4 billion US dollars.

K-pop is a cultural revolution that began in the 1990s, intended specifically for a foreign market. Its purpose was to spread an awareness of Korean culture around the world and act as a kind of *soft diplomacy*--a way of gaining power and influence in the East Asian community of nations. That strategy has worked.

> "K-pop's contribution to the Korean economy each year is a staggering 4 billion US dollars."

K-pop is a mixture of pop bands, synchronized dancing, TV dramas, and the Korean lifestyle. It appears in cosmetics, fashion, and advertising Everything Korean is a part of the Korean Wave.

"Korea Fever": October 2012 cover of Bangkok's TV Guide.

Vocabulary

- **state...art**: the latest, most recent high-tech
- **to take in**: earn, accumulate money
- **sale...abroad**: selling Korean products in foreign countries
- **staggering**: almost too much to imagine, an extremely large amount
- **gaining...nations**: achieving a more important role among Asian countries
- **synchronized dancing**: all the dancers do the same move at the same time
- **Everything Korean**: anything related to Korea or Korean culture

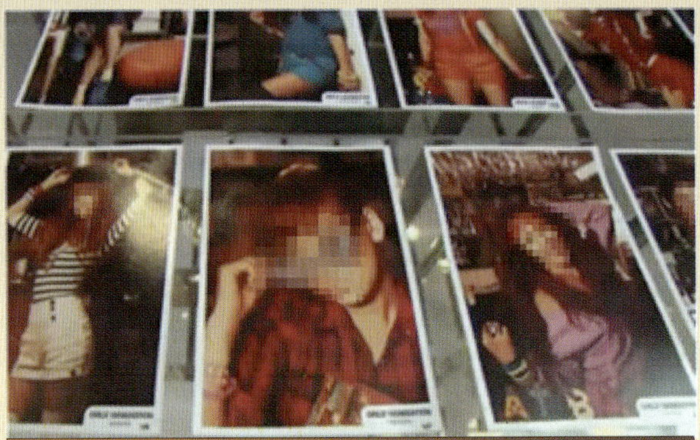

Taking idol worship to an extreme: posters of Korean pop stars at a cosmetic surgery clinic.

Korea pop has been very successful in achieving its goal of making Korea a household word all over Asia.

Rapidly developing Thailand, which looks up to Korea as its role model, calls it "Korea Fever". Bangkok department stores hold month-long "Korea Festivals" during which time they promote Korean products and culture. Kimchee is sold in every supermarket, and Korean pop music is all over Thai TV.

Korean pop stars are as well known in some Asian countries as they are in Korea. And while this interest in Korea pop stars is flattering to Koreans, it is idol worship that borders on bizarre. Not only do fans copy those stars' fashions and hair styles, but Asian women are even traveling to Korea for cosmetic surgery so that they can look like their favorite Korean pop stars!

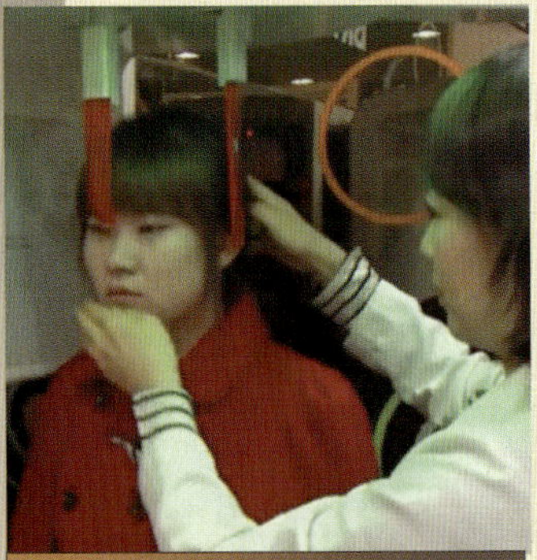

Cosmetic surgery to look like a Korean pop star.

As strange as that may sound, there's more. K-pop is a totally manufactured phenomenon. Nothing is real. Everything is created and controlled by marketing agencies—even the pop bands themselves. They are products made for export, the same as Korean electronics and cars.

A perfect example would be the 7-member girl group Rania, which is a collection of seven young women, who were interviewed for the job and were chosen specifically for their good looks and 170 cm. height.

Peruvian magazine cover

Vocabulary

- **a...word**: everybody knows about Korea
- **to look up to**: envy, idolize, respect
- **(be) all over**: can be seen often, appears a lot
- **idol worship**: to make them into gods, want to be them
- **borders...bizarre**: too strange for words, doesn't seem natural
- **chosen...height**: Only very beautiful and very tall girls could be in the group.

As successful as K-pop has been in revitalizing the Korean economy following the disastrous 1997 Asian economic crisis, some Koreans are not impressed.

- **Lacks Originality**. K-pop was patterned after US pop music in the 1990s, so they say it's foreign, not a reflection of Korean culture or values.
- **Destroying Traditional Korean Arts**. Is is possible that this foreign-inspired entertainment could be the death knell for traditional Korean culture?
- **It's Fake** K-pop bands are designed and controlled by entertainment agencies, not by the artists. Entertainers are just employees who can be fired.
- **Incites Teen Gang Violence**: Sometimes people get hurt at K-pop events, such as when a 2012 Gangnam-Style dancing competition in Bangkok imitating K-pop star Psy's popular video, turned ugly and shots were fired.

The question many people are asking now is, how long can it last? In today's fast-changing global market, even K-pop insiders know that unless it is diversified, people will start to lose interest.

Will K-pop kill traditional Korean arts?

Boy band

Philippine prison inmates dance Gangnam style

Vocabulary

- **to revitalize**: make it strong and healthy again
- **(be) patterned after**: try to imitate, be just the same as...
- **(be) the death knell**: be the thing that will destroy it
- **fake**: not genuine, an imitation
- **to turn ugly**: some kind of violence, fighting, etc. began
- **to last**: go on, to continue (to be popular)
- **(be) diversified**: change, not stay exactly the same

K-pop superstar Psy's "Gangnam Style" video is YouTube's 'most watched' video

WORD PRACTICE

Fill in the correct word.

1. K-Pop is a____revolution that started in the 1990s.
2. Thailand____up to Korea as its rags-to-riches____model.
3. K-Pop is a mixture of singing and____dancing.
4. K-Pop has made Korea a____word in many Asian countries.
5. Interest in Korean pop stars borders on____worship.
6. Pop dancers have to____their dancing all day long.
7. K-Pop has truly helped to____the Korean economy.
8. K-Pop was____after American pop music of the '90s.
9. A Gangnam-Style concert in Bangkok turned____.

a. synchronized
b. idol
c. patterned
d. looks
e. role
f. revitalize
g. ugly
h. cultural
i. rehearse
j. household

Answers on page 160.

DISCUSS

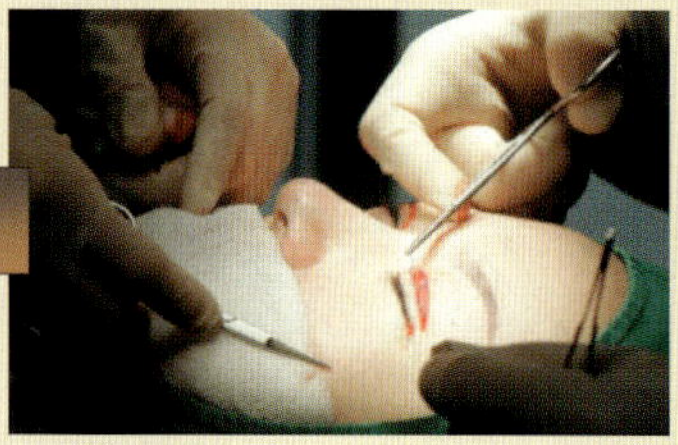

Cosmetic surgery

1. What's your general opinion of K-pop? Tell why you think so.
   - I love it.
   - It's ridiculous.
   - I have no interest in K-pop.
2. How about foreign women having cosmetic surgery to look like Korean pop stars?
   - Very flattering that they want to look like Koreans.
   - Very silly, very immature to change your face to look like a pop star.
3. Should pop stars have to give permission if someone wants to copy their face through cosmetic surgery? Tell why you think so.
4. Do you agree that K-pop is having a negative effect on traditional Korean arts? Will traditional Korean culture eventually be destroyed by K-pop?
   - No, that won't happen. Traditional Korean arts will never be replaced by K-pop.
   - I think it's possible. Young people are losing interest in traditional Korean arts.
5. What do you think about the fact that K-pop groups are formed and controlled by entertainment agencies? Doesn't that make these bands less "real" than groups formed by artists themselves?
6. How about the fact that the agencies control every aspect of the performers' lives, not allowing them to visit family or friends or have boyfriends or cell phones? Isn't that a little too much control over their personal lives, or is it necessary for success?
7. What do you think about the fact that K-pop is money-driven, that profits are more important than the welfare of the performers?
8. What is the future of K-pop? Will it last for many years, or is it just a fad that will fade? Tell why you think so.

Jordan's Queen Rania

9. Girl group Rania is a perfect example of an artificial K-pop group, composed of 7 girls, each unusually beautiful and exactly 170 cm. tall. The group was named after Queen Rania of Jordan because she is so beautiful. Is there anything about those details that seems strange to you?
10. In order to expand the Korean Wave into more countries, here are some actions being
    - Composing songs in other languages
    - Giving groups names in the local languages
    - Adding more non-Korean band members
    - Creating a Korean superstar like Michael Jackson to conquer the world

Lifestyle

UNIT 13

Learning English in Korea

Realizing that Korea's future prosperity would depend a lot on its English communication skills, the Korean government began to place the highest priority on English education in the mid-1990s. President Kim Young Sam made "globalization" a household word and emphasized that Korea's English communication skills would have to be improved if the country was ever going to play an important role in the world marketplace.

At the same time the emergence of the Internet and the growing reliance on telecommunications worldwide made it clear that some drastic changes in Korea's English education policy would have to be made.

Almost overnight the emphasis shifted away from teaching written English to spoken English. The college entrance exam was revised to focus more on listening and comprehension than grammar.

> "...the Korean government began to place the highest priority on English education..."

Today Korea is the only country in Asia outside of Singapore and the Philippines where English is taught as a core subject in the early grades of elementary school. In all other Asian countries, English instruction begins during the 1st year of middle school, when students are already 12 years old.

English class for little kids

Lifestyle

Vocabulary

- **prosperity**: wealth
- **place...on**: make it the most important thing
- **globalization**: all countries of the world interacting together
- **household word**: something that everybody knows about
- **emergence**: beginning, entry into the world of communications
- **reliance (on)**: being dependent on
- **to shift...from**: change the emphasis from
- **core subject**: a required subject that all students must learn, same as math and science

English is the language of international business.

English speaking ability has been essential for getting a job with any of the major multinational corporations in Korea since the 1990s. Job applicants have to pass oral interviews in English, which are usually conducted by native speakers, in order to be considered for important positions. Today it is impossible for a college graduate with no English conversation ability to land a good job with a major corporation in Korea.

Another driving force in Korea's push for better English communication ability has been the increasing importance of email in conducting business. Company salesmen and other representatives who can't communicate orally in English can't write impressive sounding emails either. People tend to write the same way that they speak, so if their spoken English is lousy, their emails will sound just as bad.

Poor English, whether spoken or written in emails, can very easily cause misunderstandings. Poorly written emails can come across as rude or even offensive if words or expressions are used in the wrong way. There is something called "business netiquette", which is a set of rules that should be followed in order not to offend anybody. Anyone who doesn't have a good command of English isn't going to be able to follow those rules.

English ability is a minimum requirement for a job at multinational Hyundai Corp.

Vocabulary

- **multinational corporations**: companies that operate in many foreign countries
- **be...for**: possibly be hired for
- **to land**: to acquire, be successful in getting
- **push**: drive, attempt to achieve
- **impressive...emails**: emails that give a good impression of the company
- **lousy**: slang word meaning "not good at all", really bad
- **come across**: give the impression of being
- **offensive**: insulting, make someone get angry
- **command**: ability to use the language well

Foreign travel is impossible without some ability to communicate in English.

Still another reason why ability to communicate in English has become more important to Koreans is that foreign travel or study abroad is very difficult without it. After restrictions on travel were lifted in 1989, Koreans began to travel in record numbers. Today it's hard to find a Korean who hasn't already traveled outside the country.

Most travel is done in SE Asia, destinations like Guam, which provides a touch of the USA for the hordes of Korean newlyweds who book their honeymoons there, Singapore, Vietnam, or Thailand, all within a few hours by plane. The more adventurous go to the USA, Canada, Australia, or even Europe, but no matter where anybody goes, ability to communicate in English is required.

For all of the reasons mentioned, English has taken on an increasingly greater role in the lives of Koreans. Koreans see English as their key to success. Korean parents who can afford it are sending their children to study abroad or enrolling them in English-only schools in Korea.

Private English language institutes (hagwons) are a booming business in Korea. There are even English classes for toddlers 3 or 4 years old.

But not everybody in Korea is convinced that starting English education that young is a good idea. There is now a movement to begin teaching English from age 10 because some people think that little kids don't need to learn English.

Artist's concept of Jeju Global Education City in Seoguipo after it is completed.

Lifestyle

Vocabulary

- **(be) lifted**: be ended, discontinued
- **in record numbers**: more than ever before, unprecedented large number
- **a...USA**: where visitors can experience the lifestyle of the USA
- **hordes**: large numbers of
- **to book**: make plane, hotel, car rental reservations
- **(be) adventurous**: not afraid to experience new things in faraway places
- **booming**: very successful
- **toddlers**: small children 2 to 4 years of age

WORD PRACTICE

Fill in the correct word.

1. Korea's future____depends a lot on its ability to use English.
2. The Korean government puts a high____on English education.
3. The 1990s saw the____of the Internet.
4. English is a____subject in the Philippines.
5. Poorly written emails can come across as rude or ____.
6. A sales representative must have a good____of English.
7. He can write okay, but his spelling is____.
8. Restrictions on travelling were____in 1989.
9. There are English classes for____ 2 to 4 years old.

a. command
b. core
c. lifted
d. lousy
e. lifted
f. priority
g. toddlers
h. emergence
i. offensive
j. prosperity

Answers on page 160.

DISCUSS

Lifestyle

1. How do you feel about learning English? Tell why you think so.
   - It's fun.
   - It's too hard. I don't like to learn English.
   - It's not too hard, but I hate learning foreign languages.
2. How important is English conversation ability to success in today's world?
   - It's very important. A person who can't speak English can't succeed in Korea.
   - It's important, but you can still get a good job without knowing English.
   - Whichever university a person graduated from is more important than English ability.
3. Compare the English language education at Korean public schools, colleges and universities and language institutes. Which one does the best job of teaching students to speak English? Tell why you think so.
4. Why do you think that Korea is the only Asian country outside of Singapore (where English is an official language) and the Philippines (that used to be part of the USA) that teaches English in the elementary school? Tell why you think so.
   - Koreans are more diligent than other Asians.
   - Koreans realize the importance of English more than other Asians do.
   - Koreans want to get ahead of (be better than) the Japanese.
5. There has been discussion about making English one of the official languages of Jeju. What do you think of that? Tell why you think so.
6. What do you think about English-speaking communities being built in Incheon and Jeju? What effect would all English-speaking cities inside Korea have on the Korean culture? Tell why you think so.
   - It will be the first step toward making Korea the 3rd Asian country, after Singapore and the Philippines, where English is an official language.
   - Not good. It will change Korean culture too much.
7. What do you think about parents sending their young children abroad to study? Good idea or not?
8. Could English someday replace Korean as the primary language of Korea? Why or why not?
9. If every Korean could speak English, would that be a good thing or a bad thing? Tell why you think so.

Source: www.koreatimes.co.kr.

UNIT 14

A Penchant for Luxury

Luxury imports jumped from 6% to 25% of total cars sold in just 5 years.

Something happened to Korean humility on the country's journey from rags to riches—it got lost. Whatever happened to the generations-old Korean tradition of making do with less, the result of the 35-year Japanese occupation and having to rebuild from the ashes of war? It was replaced by a penchant for extravagance.

Credit card debt in modern day Korea has soared to a crisis level because very few Koreans are willing to wait to get what they want. If they don't have the money to buy it, they just charge it. According to a report released by the Bank of Korea in 2007, household debt was a total of 582 trillion won (US$614 billion), up 11.7% from the year before.

But what is really making the problem even worse is that a big chunk of the money being spent today is not for necessities of life but rather for luxury goods—things that any reasonable person can easily do without.

"Unfortunately, it's getting hard to find a reasonable Korean"

Unfortunately, it's getting hard to find a reasonable Korean. In 2002 imported luxury cars accounted for only 6% of large car sales, but by 2006 the percentage had risen to 25%.

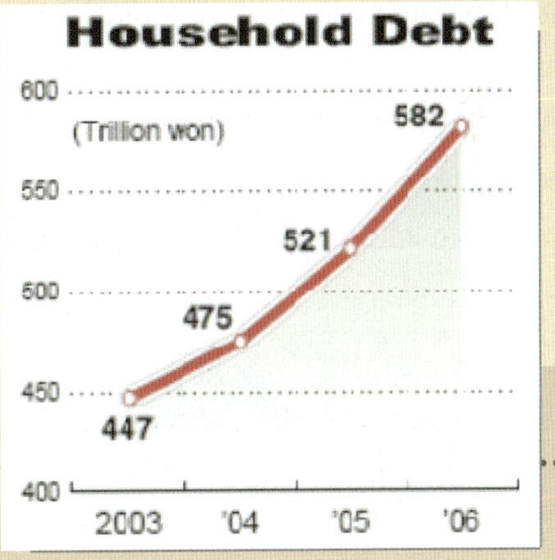

Vocabulary

- **making...less**: living on less money
- **rebuild...war**: complete recovery from the damage caused by war
- **penchant...extravagance**: preferring to have expensive things
- **soared...level**: has become extremely serious
- **to charge it**: buy on credit, pay for it with a credit card.
- **household debt**: total amount of money owed by all the members of a family
- **necessities...life**: the basic needs, such as food, housing, clothing
- **to do without**: things you really don't need, things you can live without

Lifestyle

Myongdong shopping district in Seoul

Seoul's Myongdong is now ranked as the world's 9th most expensive place to shop for clothes. Besides Myongdong, the shopper with money to burn can also have a ball shopping for luxury goods in Apkujong or Chongdam dongs. That's quite a remarkable turnaround for a country where just one generation ago the average Korean spent his or her time at shijangs haggling over the price of a pair of socks costing 50 won.

That may still be true for some older Koreans, but it would be hard to find any trendy Korean who would prefer to wear something that costs less. Today the thinking is, the more expensive, the better.

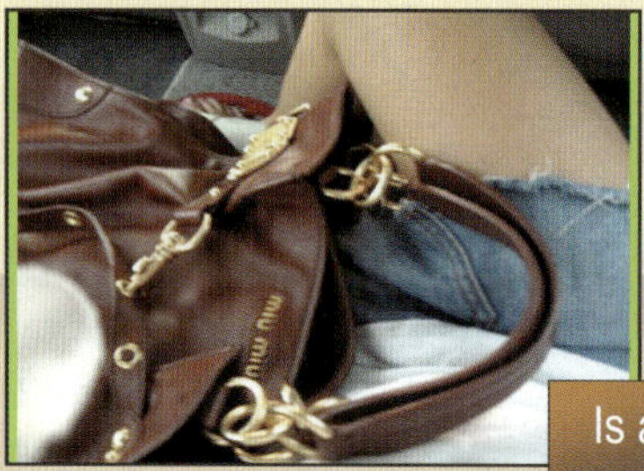
Is any handbag worth 1,000,000 won?

The latest trend among students graduating from Korea's top ranked universities is to throw lavish graduation parties attended by thousands of people at luxury hotels.

> "A generation ago the average Korean spent time at a shijang haggling over the price of a pair of socks costing 50 won."

Tourists returning from trips abroad used to come home with bottles of expensive whiskey, but today they bring back golf clubs, Gucci handbags and Rolex wristwatches costing thousands of dollars. Koreans can't seem to get enough luxury goods to satisfy their appetites.

Boutiques are filled with things that nobody needs.

Vocabulary

- **with...burn**: have a lot of money to spend on unnecessary things
- **have a ball (or blast)**: have a wonderful time, a lot of fun
- **turnaround**: reversal, the exact opposite
- **to haggle**: to argue to try and get a lower price
- **trendy**: up-to-date on all the current styles and the newest fashions
- **to...lavish**: to host very expensive...
- **can't...enough**: always want more and more
- **satisfy...appetites**: to have enough, not to want any more

Koreans really do have an insatiable appetite for luxury goods. That is shown by the amount of luxury goods confiscated by Korean customs officials at airports. A traveler is permitted to bring in only so much duty free, but the bargain prices in duty free shops are too good for most of them to pass up.

In 2006 Korean customs inspectors seized 13,535 mostly Gucci or Louis Vuitton handbags, 4,573 luxury watches and 7,751 articles of expensive clothing. It's unfortunate that so many Koreans spend so much time and money buying up luxury items that end up being confiscated anyway. It all amounts to so much money being tossed down the drain.

A watch like these can cost 5,000,000 won.

> "After having suffered in poverty... [Koreans] are...finally in a position to enjoy the finer things of life."

Many people have speculated about why Koreans are so turned on by luxury goods. After all, Korea is one of the fastest growing markets in the world for foreign made luxury goods. Articles have appeared in newspapers and magazines about it, and books have even been written about it.

The answer might be found in recent Korean history. After having suffered in poverty for most of the past century, they are only finally in a position to enjoy the finer things of life.

Lifestyle

Vocabulary

- **insatiable**: never able to be satisfied, always want more
- **(be) confiscated**: be taken from them
- **only...much**: just a certain specified amount and no more, there's a top limit
- **to pass up**: not buy
- **tossed...drain**: be wasted
- **(be) turned on (by)...**: to really like something very much
- **the...life**: nice, expensive things

WORD PRACTICE

Fill in the correct word.

1. Modern-day Koreans truly do have a____for extravagance.
2. They have an____appetite for luxury goods.
3. A generation ago Koreans were used to making____with less.
4. The money being spent is not for the____of life.
5. People with money to____can have a____shopping at Apkujong.
6. Trendy Koreans aren't interested in____over prices at shijangs.
7. College graduates are now throwing____parties at____hotels.
8. Tons of luxury goods are____by Customs officers at the airports.

a. confiscated
b. lavish
c. blast
d. penchant
e. haggling
f. necessities
g. luxury
h. insatiable
i. burn
j. do

Answers on page 160.

DISCUSS

Lifestyle

1960

1. What can explain why Koreans, who were poor just one generation ago now have very expensive tastes in clothes and luxury goods? What has caused them to change so much so fast? Tell why you think so.
2. It has been said that Koreans, like the Chinese, like to show off how much money they have by buying expensive things. Do you agree with that? If so, why do they think like that? What is the historical background (reason) for that kind of thinking?
3. The accumulation of credit card debt has reached a crisis level in Korea in recent years. Why have Koreans, who used to prefer to save money rather than spend it, become so dependent on credit cards? Why have so many Koreans allowed themselves to fall into debt? Tell why you think so.

4. What is your own experience with credit cards? Do you often charge things, or do you always buy things with cash? If so, why?
5. Most Koreans would rather buy something that costs more than buy something that costs less. In other words, the higher the price, the better. Have Koreans always felt that way, or is this something new? Why do Koreans prefer to buy expensive things?
   - Koreans have always wanted to show off their money to other people.
   - Koreans have always liked expensive things.
   - Koreans enjoy spending money.
6. What's the best way to solve the problem of Korean travelers bringing in more duty free items than the law permits? Tell why you think so.
   - Make the penalties more severe, make them lose the items plus pay a fine.
   - Change the law. Let travelers bring in more things.
   - Put a limit on how much money travelers can spend in foreign countries.
7. What do you think of throwing lavish college graduation parties at luxury hotels? Do you think that's a good trend or something that should be stopped? Tell why you think so.
8. How is the Korean economy affected by Koreans spending too much money on foreign made luxury goods? Is there a point where the government should do something to try and stop it? Why or why not?
9. How do Koreans compare with the Japanese and the Chinese in regard to spending money on imported luxury goods? Do they spend more or less? Tell why you think so.

UNIT 15

The Love Hotels

Love hotels have been a source of controversy ever since the first one opened up in the 1980s. Many people in Korea find these business establishments not only morally objectionable but a blight on Korean culture. They also blame them for the increasing promiscuity in the society by providing everyone a convenient place to go and have sex.

Similar to flop houses, love hotels are easily recognized by the plastic curtains that hang at the entrances of their parking lots. The plastic curtains are there so that the people going inside to carry on their secret love affairs can't be seen from the road when they get in or out of their cars. The rooms are usually rented by the hour, but they can also be rented overnight. There are thousands of love hotels across the country, over 400 in Seoul alone.

> "There are...over 400 love hotels in Seoul alone"

In the late 1990s a large number of love hotels sprang up in the bedroom communities surrounding Seoul, namely Ilsan, Bundang, and Seongnam, angering the residents of those upscale communities. They especially didn't like the fact that many love hotels were built near schools. It was too much for local residents to take, and so large demonstrations broke out.

Parking entrance of the "Palace of Dreams" love hotel, across the street from a high school.

Vocabulary

- **morally objectionable**: not acceptable for reasons of morality
- **a blight**: stain, black mark
- **promiscuity**: having sex with many different sex partners
- **flop houses**: houses of prostitution, places only for having sex
- **bedroom communities**: housing areas where people who work in the city live
- **upscale**: more expensive, more desirable places to live
- **too...take**: they couldn't endure it

Lifestyle

The fact that love hotels have been built near schools has been the main objection of the opponents of the love hotels. Without any regard to the children who had to walk past them everyday, some owners built motels right across the street from schools.

The demonstrations that occurred in the 1990s caught the attention of people all across the country, and the subject of love hotels became a national issue. Restrictions were placed on where love hotels could be built, and some towns even passed laws banning love hotels altogether.

> [Love hotels were]...designed as places for married couples with children...to have sex.

Opponents of love hotels took their fight to the Internet by taking pictures of the license plates of cars going in and out of the love hotel parking lots. They also took pictures of the people getting in and out of the cars and posted them online.

Typical Korean love hotel

Many Koreans don't realize it, but the concept of love hotels actually came from Japan. Love hotels became popular in Japan in the 1970s but didn't make their way into Korea until the mid-80s.

Although love hotels are convenient places for married people to cheat on their spouses, they were originally designed as places for married couples living in small houses with children or parents to have sex.

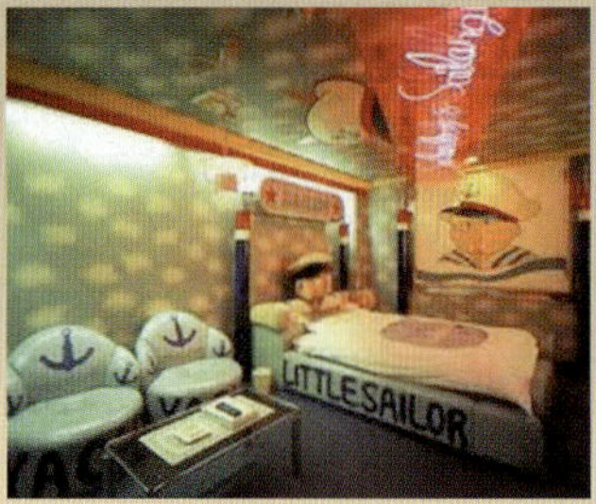

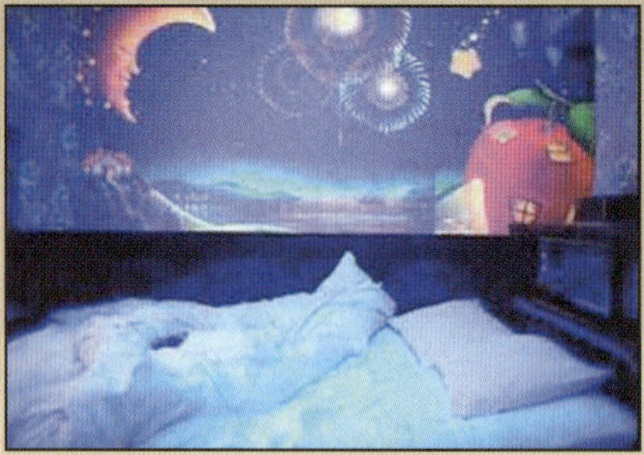

Expensive love hotels with "theme" rooms.

Vocabulary

- **caught...of**: make them become aware of it
- **took...Internet**: use the Internet to spread their views
- **cheat...spouses**: have sex with other people besides their husbands or wives

Korean love hotels vary drastically in terms of quality and pricing. Low end love hotels are a lot like ordinary yogwans. They are as plain on the outside as they are on the inside. But the biggest difference between a cheap love hotel and a yogwan is that love hotels have hourly rates but yogwans don't. People don't check into yogwans for just a few hours.

A round love hotel bed

> Mirrors on walls and ceiling, and round beds.

High end love hotels could never be mistaken for regular hotels because of the flashing lights and neon signs that adorn their exteriors.

The rooms inside the love hotels look nothing like normal hotel rooms. Rooms are elaborately decorated with mirrors on the walls, sometimes also on the ceiling, and the beds are either round or follow some type of theme.

Car sex?

The themes carry into the bathrooms, which are sometimes almost as large as the bedrooms. The rooms and baths have every conceivable convenience anybody could want. In the rooms there are hair dryers, coffee pots with coffee and tea, and refrigerators are stocked with drinks and a variety of snack foods. Condoms are always provided.

While many of these same things can also be found in regular Korean hotel rooms, love hotel rooms have one thing that can't be found in regular hotels—a TV channel running pornographic movies 24 hours a day.

Love motels have colorful exteriors.

Lifestyle

Vocabulary

- **vary drastically**: a huge range from top to bottom
- **low end**: inexpensive, low quality (opposite: high end)
- **be mistaken for**: have somebody think it's a hotel and not a love hotel
- **to adorn**: decorate (be decorated with)
- **(be) elaborately decorated**: very fancy, not plain and simple
- **every...convenience**: all the things to make their stay comfortable
- **(be) stocked with**: have available inside
- **(be) running**: showing, playing

WORD PRACTICE

Fill in the correct word.

1. Many Koreans find love hotels morally____.
2. They are blamed for the increased____in the society.
3. ____communities do not want love hotels anywhere near them.
4. Love hotels are similar to____houses.
5. The demos of the 90s made love hotels a national____.
6. They caught the____of people all over the country.
7. They are places where married people can____on their____.
8. The rooms are well____with snack foods and condoms.
9. Some rooms are____decorated with mirrors on the ceiling.

a. upscale
b. objectionable
c. attention
d. stocked
e. spouses
f. issue
g. promiscuity
h. elaborately
i. flop
j. cheat

Answers on page 160.

DISCUSS

1. What do you think of love hotels? Which of these statements do you agree with and why?
   - They are okay. People need a nice place to have sex.
   - Love hotels are not good. They should all be closed down.
2. What percentage of love hotel clients are married couples and what percentage are people cheating on their spouses?
3. Do you think there should be any restrictions on where love hotels can be built? Should people have the right to build a love hotel anywhere they want to? Why or why not?
4. How would you feel if a love hotel was built near your child's school? Would you demonstrate to have it closed down or have it moved to another place? Why or why not?
5. How would you feel if a love hotel was built next door to your house? Would that be okay? If not, why not?
6. What do you think of taking pictures of license plates or the faces of people going in and out of love hotels and posting them on the Internet? Is that a good way to stop people from using love hotels? Why or why not?
7. What's your opinion of prostitution, which is currently illegal in Korea? Should prostitution be legalized? Why or why not?
8. Do you think that love hotels are partly responsible for the increase of promiscuity among Korean teenagers? Are love hotels at least partly to blame? Tell why you think so.
9. Which of the following groups do you think make up the majority of love hotel customers? Tell why you think so.
   - Married couples who can't have sex at home
   - Married men and women cheating on their spouses
   - Unmarried people who want to have sex after going on a date
   - College students or high school students
10. What about love hotel owners? What kind of people operate love hotels? Why don't they open up regular hotels for families?
11. In surveys, teenagers as young as 14 have said they had sex in a yogwan.
    a. Should there be a minimum age for checking into a yogwan or love hotel?
    b. What kind of a yogwan owner would allow teenagers to check into rooms?
    c. What kind of punishment, if any, should there be for yogwan or love hotel owners who allow teenagers to rent their rooms?

Lifestyle

UNIT 16

Fashion Awareness

Anybody who visited Korea in 1982 and then came back today for a second look would think that their plane had landed in the wrong country. They would not recognize the place, and they certainly wouldn't recognize the people. The difference between the way Koreans looked back then and the way Koreans look today is striking.

Koreans in the early 80s were a poor, hard working group of people. Their country was still getting over the ravages of war, still led by dictatorship governments, but starting to get on its feet economically. Life was very hard and filled with inconveniences, and Koreans had a lot more important things to think about than how they dressed.

"Koreans are...among the most fashion-conscious people in all of Asia."

Fast forward to the 21st century and it is like the difference between night and day. Not only are Koreans very well dressed, but they are among the most fashion-conscious people in all of Asia. Some of the best fashion boutiques in the Far East are found in Seoul's Myongdong and Kangnam areas.

Kangnam: a mecca for the fashion-aware

Lifestyle

Vocabulary

- **striking**: very noticeable
- **get...economically**: improve its economic situation, stop being a poor country
- **fast forward**: contrast that (long ago) period to today
- **the...day**: so different as to be complete opposites
- **fashion-conscious**: think very much about styles and fashion
- **boutiques**: expensive shops selling very expensive clothing and accessories
- **mecca**: a perfect place, a paradise

The Korean fashion industry is renowned the world over, and Koreans are among the best customers. But even more popular with fashion-conscious Koreans are the designer brands sold in shops that line the streets and alleyways of Myongdong, Apgujeong, and Cheongdam dongs. Enormous sums of money are spent in those shops every day.

The surge in demand for designer clothing began in the 1990s. For the first time ever, Koreans had money to spend, and spend they did, much to the dismay of the Korean government. Spending a lot of money on luxury goods, of which designer clothing is included, is bad for the Korean economy because it results in too much money leaving the country.

However, pleas from the government to hold down the spending on luxury designer goods have fallen on deaf ears. Koreans, especially Korean women, are often described in foreign publications as a "designer-label obsessed people".

Korean women are described as "designer-label obsessed".

But not all designer goods are imported. There are Korean designer labels too, and they are just as popular as the imported stuff. The main thing is that Koreans want designer labels. If something isn't "designer", they won't buy it.

Vocabulary

- **renowned...over**: famous all over the world
- **surge in demand**: sudden popularity
- **dismay**: disappointment, frustration
- **pleas**: begging, strong requests
- **hold down**: keep it to a minimum, don't do it so much
- **fallen...ears**: they didn't listen, ignored the pleas
- **(be) obsessed (with)**: that's all they want, to have an excessive interest in...

Besides the fact that designer clothing is very expensive, the price is even higher when considering that clothes go out of style very quickly. Since clothing styles change every year or so, the money spent on clothes last year is money down the drain if those clothes can't be worn this year.

Offsetting that disadvantage while allowing the fashion-conscious to keep up with the latest styles is something new called "fast fashion"—the latest designer styles but made cheaply. It doesn't last more than a year.

Fast fashion has really caught on in Korea. More and more chain stores are rushing to fill the demand for this type of inexpensive yet ultra-fashionable clothing.

From the standpoint of the fashion-conscious, the benefit of fast fashion over designer labels is obvious—being able to keep up with the latest clothing styles without having to throw away much money.

Unfortunately, fast fashion has turned into an environmental issue because it encourages waste. People throw away their used clothing instead of passing them down, contributing to the pollution of the earth. According to a report issued by the Korean Salvation Army in March of 2007 it takes 30 years for thrown away garments to be absorbed by the earth. If they are burned, they add more pollutants to the air.

"Fast fashion" has been a huge success in Korea.

Vocabulary

- **go...style**: become old-fashioned
- **down...drain**: wasted, thrown away
- **to offset**: to lessen, make it not so bad
- **to catch on**: to become popular
- **ultra-fashionable**: the very latest style
- **From...of**: according to the way that they see it, in their opinion
- **passing...down**: giving them to someone else, such as a younger sibling
- **garments**: articles of clothing

WORD PRACTICE

Fill in the correct word.

1. The difference between today and 20 years ago is____.
2. Koreans are among the most fashion-____in all of Asia.
3. Some of the world's finest____are in Myongdong.
4. The Korean fashion industry is____the whole world over.
5. The government's____to cut spending falls on____ears.
6. Koreans have the reputation of being____with designer labels.
7. The problem is that clothes go out of____very fast.
8. Fast fashion has really____on in Korea.
9. A lot of money spent on clothing is thrown down the____.

a. pleas
b. renowned
c. obsessed
d. conscious
e. caught
f. boutiques
g. drain
h. striking
i. style
j. deaf

Answers on page 160.

Lifestyle

DISCUSS

1. Do you agree that Koreans are "obsessed" with designer labels? Do Koreans, especially young people, care if their clothes have designer labels or not? If so, why do they care?
2. What do you think of people who spend a lot of time thinking about fashion and clothing styles? Tell why you think so.
   a. They're crazy. Spending a lot of money on clothes is a waste of time and money.
   b. They're smart. Other people judge you by the clothes that you wear.
3. What is the main reason why Koreans buy designer clothing? Tell why you think so.
   a. They're mostly concerned about quality. They want to wear well-made clothes.
   b. They're mostly concerned with the labels. They want to show off to other people.
4. How would you describe the average Korean's attitude toward their personal appearance? Tell why you think so.
   a. Most Koreans don't care much about their appearance or about clothing styles.
   b. Most Koreans care very much about how they look and about the clothes they wear.
5. How do you think young Koreans compare to young people in Japan when it comes to caring about clothes, fashions, and designer labels? Tell why you think so.
   a. Koreans are probably more fashion-conscious than the Japanese.
   b. The Japanese are probably more fashion-conscious than Koreans.
   c. They're both about the same when it comes to fashion awareness.
6. Are you one of those people who likes to wear designer clothes? Do you have any designer clothes? If so, why did you buy them? If you don't have any, why not?
7. Don't you agree that spending big money on (designer) clothes that will soon go out of style is just like throwing money away? Why or why not?
8. Have you ever heard of fast fashion? Do you think it's a good idea? Have you bought any fast fashion clothing?
9. Isn't it true that fast fashion encourages waste and pollution of the environment? Is there any way to protect the environment while letting people keep up with the latest clothes styles?
10. Would you wear clothes that were "last year's style"? Why or why not? Would you ever wear any used clothing? Why or why not?

Fast fashion for men

UNIT 17

Marriage and Divorce

Korea's divorce rate increased by 900% over a period of just 20 years. In 1983 only 5% of Korean marriages ended in divorce, but by 2003 the rate had risen to a whopping 47%. Korea's divorce rate doubled between 1995 and 2006. 370 Korean couples ended their marriage each day in 2009. That comes to a total of 11,100 divorces per month.

In the early 80s Korea's divorce rate was one of the lowest in the world, but now it is one of highest in Asia, just after Japan. That's a remarkable about face for a country where divorce was almost unheard of one generation before.

What could have happened in Korean society to cause its divorce rate to go through the roof in just one generation? One thing that happened is that Korean parent-arranged marriages became obsolete.

"370 Korean couples ended their marriage each day in 2009".

No longer obligated to respect their parents' wishes in terms of who they should be married to, modern Korean couples are no longer willing to stay in marriages that go bad.

The result is a high divorce rate that nobody could have imagined in their wildest dreams.

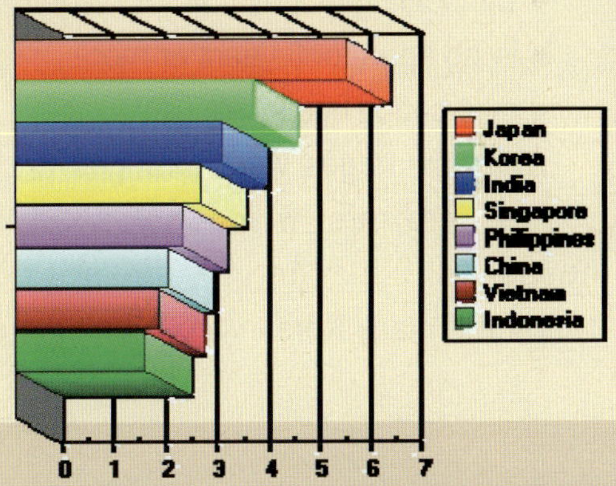

Asian divorces: Korea is second highest.

Lifestyle

Vocabulary

- **a...47%**: **whopping** implies that 47% is extremely high
- **(an) about face**: **about face** is a military command to turn to the opposite direction
- **(be) unheard of**: something that never happens
- **go...roof**: implies that it went extremely high
- **(be) obligated**: feel a sense of duty, an obligation
- **could...dreams**: impossible to imagine ever happening

TV drama about married life originally titled, "Ihon-haji mapshida" (Let's not divorce).

Any one of the following conditions qualify as a valid reason for filing for a divorce in Korea:

- adultery
- unreasonable behavior
- excessive drinking
- making unreasonable sexual demands
- neglect
- withholding money from the other
- living apart for 3 years or more
- mistreating one's in-laws

When marriages were arranged and divorces were rare, women tolerated their husbands' philandering, but no more. Nowadays many Korean women hit the ceiling if their husbands even look at another woman, and sometimes they don't even have to look. All a husband has to do is come home late from work a few times to convince his wife that he's having an extra-marital affair.

Women still file for more divorces than men, but the number of men filing for divorce has been rising. Most men give personality differences as the reason for wanting a divorce. That's not surprising considering that most couples today rush into marriage without spending much time getting to know one another.

The most popular method of finding a husband or wife in Korea today is by attending a "meeting", which is a blind date arranged by family or friends. That's because they're too busy to find a husband or wife by themselves.

But all too often, in their eagerness to get married, they start making wedding plans after just a few dates, only to find themselves in divorce court a couple of years later.

Vocabulary

- **adultery**: having sex with someone other than the husband or wife
- **neglect**: ignoring the needs of your marriage partner
- **in-laws**: the husband's or wife's family
- **philandering**: having love affairs with other men or women
- **to hit...ceiling**: become extremely angry, often violently so
- **extramarital affair**: love affair outside of the marriage (extra-marital)
- **to rush...marriage**: make the decision to get married too soon
- **blind date**: a date when the dating partner has never been met before

The drastic increase in divorces in the country set off alarm bells with Korean lawmakers, and in 2003 they decided to try and do something about it. To prevent divorces resulting from fits of anger, a law was passed requiring a 1-week cooling off period from the time a divorce suit was filed.

Passing the law was a wise move because it proved to be very effective in lowering the divorce rate. It was even more effective than counseling. In 2006 the deliberation period was extended to 3 weeks, and the divorce rate fell even more. The new law lowered the number of divorces in Korea by 25%, from a peak of 167,000 in 2003 to 127,000 in 2006.

In 2005 the Korean parliament took a huge step to lower the divorce rate by revising the century-old Civil Law which stated that only males could be registered as the head of families. They decided that it was silly for a young boy without a father to be made the head of a family instead of his mother.

They also made it possible for a boy to adopt his mother's or stepfather's last name in case of a remarriage. While this has always been routine in western countries, in Korea it was a drastic reversal of traditional thinking which began with the passage of the "hojuje" law in 1898.

> "...a drastic reversal of traditional thinking that began...in 1898."

Other changes in Korea's divorce law have made the division of property more equitable instead of everything going to the husband. In most cases the property is divided 50/50 with the wife getting just as much as the husband. Whatever the husband owns, she gets half.

"Why do I get the feeling my divorce is final?"

Vocabulary

- **set...bells**: made them decide that something had to be done to stop it
- **fit of anger**: sudden and violent argument
- **cooling...period**: a time to calm down and think about it
- **a...move**: a very smart action to take
- **counseling**: sitting down and talking with an expert on marriage problems
- **deliberation period**: a time to talk it over in a calm manner
- **remarriage**: when the divorced husband or wife gets married again
- **equitable**: more equal, fairer, not favoring one more than the other

Lifestyle

WORD PRACTICE

Fill in the correct word.

1. Korea did an about____ on divorce since the '80s.
2. Divorce was____of in Korea just one generation ago.
3. Young people are no longer____to____their parents' wishes.
4. A lot of____is committed in the love hotels.
5. Wives often accuse their husbands of having____affairs.
6. Too many young Koreans____into marriage too soon.
7. A ____-off period law was first past in 2003.
8. ____after a divorce was almost unheard of 30 years ago.
9. The new divorce law makes division of property more____.

a. rush
b. adultery
c. cooling
d. unheard
e. extramarital
f. equitable
g. face
h. respect
i. remarriage
j. obligated

Answers on page 160.

DISCUSS

1. What do you think is the biggest reason for the increase in the number of divorces in Korea compared to just 20 or 25 years ago? Discuss each of these possible factors. Tell why you think so.
   - Korean women becoming more independent
   - Korean society becoming more liberal in their thinking about divorces
   - Young couples rushing into marriage too fast
   - Meeting new people online in Internet chat rooms
   - The change from arranged marriages to today's "love" marriages

2. Internet chatting has given many bored housewives a chance to meet other men online. Could this have had much of an effect on the increase in the number of divorces? Why or why not?
3. The divorce rate in Korea was very low in the days when most parents arranged marriages for their children. Why do you think there were so few divorces in those days? Tell why you think so.
4. Would you like to see the custom of arranged marriages become popular again? Why or why not?
5. How are today's "meetings" different from the old meetings arranged by parents? Considering that today's "meetings" end up in many divorces, weren't the parent-arranged meetings better? Why or why not?
6. How do you feel about the Civil Law allowing women to register as the heads of families? Tell why you think so.
   - It's good that the law was changed.
   - The old law was old-fashioned and unfair.
   - I don't like it. It doesn't seem right for females to be the heads of families.
7. What do you think about boys being allowed to adopt the last names of their mothers or stepfathers, in case their mother remarries? Tell why you think so.
   - I think it's a sensible move toward a more democratic Korean society.
   - No, I don't think a boy should be allowed to change his last name for any reason. He must keep the name of his real father, even if the father is dead.
8. People against it charge that the new Civil Law will result in the breakdown of traditional Korean family ties, but people in favor say it will finally eliminate Koreans' narrow-minded view of blood ties. Which side do you agree with? Tell why you think so.

UNIT 18

The Gender Gap

Even though Korean women have made great strides toward achieving full equality with men in the last couple of decades, they still have a long way to go in closing the gender gap. Some progress has been made in the world of business, in politics, and in the society in general, but Korean women still lag far behind men when it comes to equal treatment under the law.

This was all too plain to see in a report on the income gap in Korea that came out in early 2007. It showed that Korean men made an average of 2.87 million won per month while the salaries and wages of Korean women averaged 36.9% lower, at just 1.87 million won. A similar study showed an income gap between men and women at about 25% in the USA and just 15% in the EU.

> A high divorce rate leaves more women to raise their children without help from the fathers.

It's always been accepted that men should earn more money than women because they have families to support, but in today's world, many women find themselves in the same situation. A high divorce rate has left more women having to raise their children without any help from the fathers.

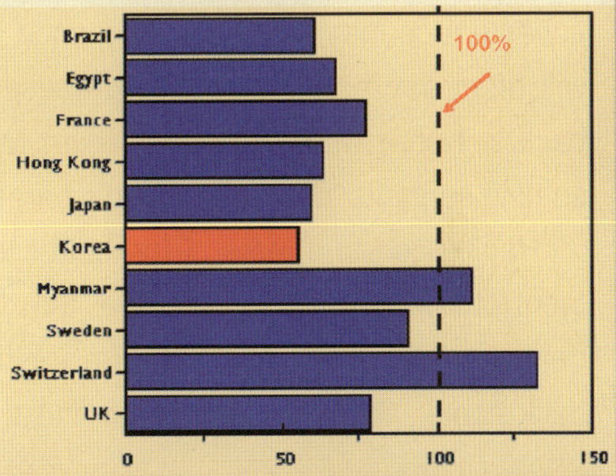

Women's Wages as a Percentage of Men's Wages (2004): Korean women earn much less than Korean men.

Vocabulary

- **have...strides**: have improved their situation
- **have...go**: still have not reached their goal
- **gender gap**: the difference between the status of men and that of women
- **equal...law**: have the same legal rights as men
- **EU**: the European Union (union of European countries)
- **find...in**: are in a situation such that...
- **raise**: support, take care of, bring up

Korean-American women enjoy freedoms women in Korea don't have.

Nobody ever had to tell Korean women about their low social standing in Korean society, but they've lately become more acutely aware of it as the result of their travels abroad. Married Korean women who have lived with their spouses in a western country for even just a short time will often say how much they dread going back to Korea where they will return to becoming servants to their husband's parents.

Having gotten a taste of the better treatment of women outside of Korea, they suddenly realize how bad things are for them back home. It is very difficult to find a Korean woman who has lived in a western country who wants to move back to Korea. That says a lot about the treatment of women in Korea.

Although some progress is being made, all of the following conditions still exist in Korea:

- **Korean women have limited job opportunities**. Even in major corporations, they are rarely given jobs of much importance. Only 0.5% of Korean women have jobs in management.
- **Divorce cases almost always end up with the children going with the father**, the opposite of what happens in the west.
- **Women not married by their late 20s are labeled "old miss"**. There is no derogatory term used for men who don't get married.
- Whenever pregnant women have abortions, the **fetuses removed are almost always female**, never male, except when the life of the mother is in danger.

Limited job opportunities.

Vocabulary

- **acutely...of**: makes them realize it even better
- **spouses**: husbands and wives
- **to dread**: hate to even think of going back, really don't want to go
- **to get...of**: have a chance to sample what it is like
- **That...lot**: We can understand the situation just from knowing that fact.
- **to be labeled**: be called, be referred to as
- **derogatory**: gives a negative impression or feeling

There have been many attempts to explain why women in Korea have a lower social standing than men, but the reason that most scholars have come up with is the Korean language itself.

When Korean women speak to men they must use a politer form of the language than Korean men use. Most Koreans assume that the gender gap goes back to Confucianism, since Confucianism puts males above females. But China is the birthplace of Confucianism, and Chinese men are not given a higher position in society than women. It happens only in Korea and Japan.

It has been suggested that maybe communism explains why there is no gender gap in China, but that's not likely. North Korea is more communist than China, but the status of women in North Korea is even lower than it is in South Korea. The only thing that sets China apart from South Korea, North Korea, and Japan is that the Chinese language has just one spoken form, used by both men and women.

A teachers meeting. 99% male.

So the general belief among sociologists is that the Korean language is the reason for the inequality of men and women in Korea. Requiring females to speak a more polite form of the language is a form of institutionalized discrimination that works to keep women in their place.

> The Korean language itself may be the reason why Korean women have lower status than men.

But things are changing. A good example of that was a 2007 court case when a 28-year-old female employee sued her boss for forcing her to go out drinking with the office staff after work. The Seoul High Court ruled that the boss violated the woman's personal rights. He was fined 2 million won and fired from the company.

Vocabulary

- **to come...with**: arrive at an answer or solution to a problem
- **to go back to**: can be explained by, be blamed on
- **(be) not likely**: that probably isn't the reason
- **institutionalized discrimination**: the inferiority of women built into the customs
- **to keep...place**: ensure that women don't get more powerful than men

WORD PRACTICE

Fill in the correct word.

1. Korean women have made great____in equality since the '80s.
2. There's still a long way to go in closing the____gap.
3. Women still don't get equal____under the law.
4. Korean women who live abroad get a____of the better life.
5. Korean women still have very____job opportunities.
6. There is no____word for men who don't get married.
7. Requiring women to speak politely to men is____discrimination.
8. It was designed to keep women in their____.
9. The language could be the cause of the lower____of women.

a. gender
b. taste
c. place
d. institutionalized
e. strides
f. status
g. treatment
h. derogatory
i. limited

Answers on page 160.

DISCUSS

Lifestyle

1. Do you agree or disagree that women in Korea have a lower position in society than men? Tell why you think so.
   - Yes, I agree that Korean society places women lower than men.
   - No, Korean men have no advantages over Korean women.
2. Do you see any difference between the way Korean women are treated today and the way they were treated when you were a child? Has been any improvement in the position of women in Korean society since then? If so, what can women do now that they couldn't do back then?
3. Do you think it's fair that the children of couples who get divorced usually go with the father? Where do you think they should go? Tell why you think so.
   - They should go with the mother. Children need mothers more than fathers.
   - They should go with the father. Only fathers can provide for them financially.
   - It depends on why they got a divorce. Fathers or mothers who cheat on their spouses should not take care of the children.
   - Do you think that women should be paid less money for doing the same job as a man? Why or why not?
4. Do you think that Korean women who don't get married by the age of 27 or 28 should be called "old miss"? Why or why not?
5. What do you think of the traditions of Korean and Japanese making women use polite language when speaking to men, but men can speak "down" to women if they want to? Isn't that unfair? Why or why not?
6. Do you agree with almost every scholar that it is the Korean language, and not Confucianism, that is responsible for keeping women inferior to men in the society? If you disagree, then how can you explain why Chinese women are on the same social level as Chinese men, even though China is the birthplace of Confucianism?
7. Was the woman (Reading 3) right or wrong to sue her boss for forcing her to go out drinking after work? What about the court's decision to fine the boss and the company's decision to fire him? Was that proper punishment for what he did?
8. Should bosses be free to force their employees—male OR female—to go out drinking with them after work? Why or why not?

Japanese women must use more polite language when speaking to men.

UNIT 19 The Quality of Life

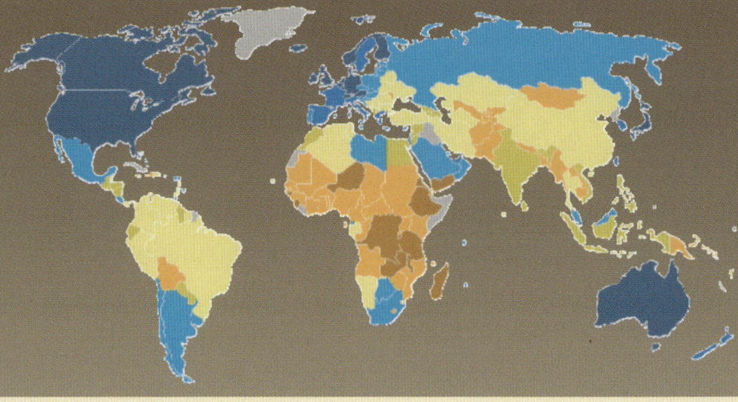

In 2012 the IMF (International Monetary Fund) ranked Luxembourg as the richest country in the world, with a per capita income of $115,000 per year. The United States was 15th with $44,000, and South Korea was No. 34, with a per capita income of $22,400.

Considering that there are 179 countries in the world, that ranking placed Koreans among the world's richest 15%, a remarkable achievement for a country that picked itself up from the ruins of war just a few decades ago. In 2007 the OECD ranked South Korea as the world's 11th largest economy and 23rd in terms of its GDP.

By all economic measurements, South Korea is a bona fide advanced country, but in reality, the quality of life in Korea is far lower than that of other advanced countries. The OECD placed Korea dead last in terms of quality of life among its 30 member countries.

> "Korea is a bona fide advanced country, but...the quality of life in Korea is far lower than any other advanced country."

Shortly after that OECD announcement President Roh Moo-hyun announced a plan to raise the standard of living in the country.

Vocabulary

- **per...income**: the nation's total income divided by the number of people
- **picked...up**: recovered
- **ruins**: complete destruction
- **bona fide**: real, genuine
- **(be) dead last**: in the very last position
- **standard...living**: the degree of comfort, convenience, and ease of living

Jams like this can't happen when everybody obeys the traffic laws.

Just having a lot of money, cars, and electronic gadgets doesn't mean a country's standard of living is high. Other important factors are things like the kind of social welfare system, if any, that is in place, how transparent business operations are, and to what degree the citizens obey the laws. In all of these areas conditions in Korea leave a lot to be desired.

Just one look at how Koreans observe traffic laws shows what they think about laws. Koreans have a lot in common with some of their Asian neighbors in believing that laws were made to be broken. Although there has been much improvement from the way things were 20 or 30 years ago, the society still has a way to go.

Koreans, and Asians in general, have their own idea of what constitutes acceptable business behavior. What they call normal most other advanced nations call corrupt. The giving of gifts in return for business favors, while common in Asia, is cause for arrest in the west.

Bribery was banned in 1953, but it continues to be a problem in Korea today. In 2001 President Kim Dae Jung, signed an anti-corruption bill into law, but nobody was willing to predict how effective it would be. Many anti-corruption laws exist in Korea, but most of them are ignored.

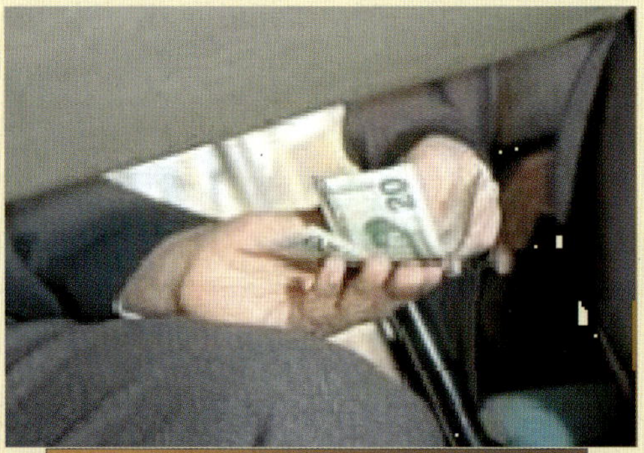

Bribery continues to be a problem.

Vocabulary

- **social...system**: government programs to help the poor, the handicapped and the elderly
- **transparent**: all details of business transactions documented and easy to verify
- **leave...desired**: need much improvement
- **have...with**: is the same as, does the same thing
- **laws...broken**: laws don't have to be obeyed
- **has...go**: not yet perfect, not yet acceptable
- **constitutes...behavior**: is the proper way to conduct business
- **(be) cause...arrest**: people can be put in prison for doing it
- **bill**: a proposed piece of legislation, before it is signed into law

Social welfare is one area where Korea really has a lot of room for improvement. Korea ranked 29th out of 30 among OECD members in terms of how much it spent on social welfare programs in 2006. The percentage of its GDP spent on welfare was just 2.4% in 2001, compared to 27% in Australia and Canada, 28% in the USA, 29% in the UK, and 42% in Sweden.

But not all the news is bad. Korea comes out at the top in many areas, particularly in terms of IT development. South Korea has the highest Internet access rate not only among OECD members but in the whole world.

Korea also spends more on education than any other OECD country, and Korean students ranked second in mathematical, scientific, and reading literacy. In terms of law, order, and defense, Korea's expenditure as a percentage of GDP was third highest in the OECD.

Koreans are also the thinnest people in the OECD, with only 3.2% of its people classified as obese. Finally, Korea ranked 4th in terms of household savings and 3rd in labor productivity.

An example of social welfare improvement in Korea. Taking care of the elderly at the Gumi Social Welfare Center

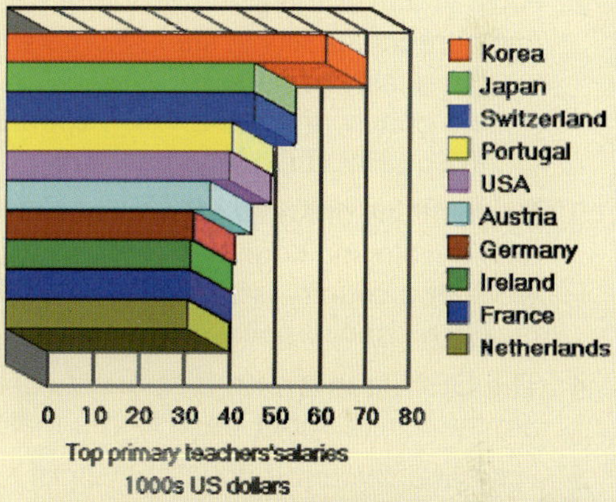

Korea has the highest primary school teachers' salaries in the world. (1999)

Data from UNESCO Institute for Statistics

Lifestyle

Vocabulary

- **room...improvement**: still not enough, needs to improve more
- **OECD**: Organization for Economic Co-operation and Development
- **IT development**: the use of technology
- **Internet...rate**: percentage of citizens who are using the Internet
- **reading literacy**: ability to read
- **expenditure**: amount of money spent
- **obese**: extremely fat
- **household savings**: the percentage of their income that a family saves
- **labor productivity**: the total amount of goods and services produced

WORD PRACTICE

Fill in the correct word.

1. Korea just picked itself up from the____of war.
2. Economically Korea is a____advanced country.
3. But Korea comes in____last in terms of quality of life.
4. Korea still doesn't have a good social____system.
5. It leaves a___to be_____.
6. Asians seem to believe that laws are made to be____,
7. In western countries giving gifts to gain favor is____for arrest.
8. Giving gifts to businessmen is____.
9. Only a tiny percentage of Koreans are classified as____.

a. desired
b. broken
c. dead
d. obese
e. cause
f. ruins
g. lot
h. bribery
i. bona fide
j. welfare

Answers on page 160.

DISCUSS

1. What do you think about the quality of life in Korea? Is it as good as it can be, or are there still some areas which make living in Korea a little inconvenient? Tell why you think so.

The quality of life is high in the west.

2. Have you ever traveled outside of Korea? If so, compare the quality in life in Korea with...
   - ...the quality of life in SE Asia
   - ...the quality of life in English-speaking countries
   - ...the quality of life in Japan
3. Do you think of Korea as an advanced country or as a developing country? How do you decide whether a country is advanced or not? What makes a country advanced?
4. The OECD ranked Korea's quality of living last among all 30 member countries. What are the things about life in Korea that may be responsible for that low ranking?
5. How would you rate the behavior of Korean drivers on the roads? Do they show consideration for other drivers, or are they selfish and inconsiderate? Do they obey traffic laws? How about yourself?
6. When you're behind the wheel, how do you behave toward other drivers? Do driving habits matter in terms of the quality of life? Why or why not?
7. What's your opinion on gift giving in business agreements? Do you think that giving money or gifts in return for favors is a good way to do business? Should there be laws against doing it? Tell why you think so.
8. Why does Korea spend so little money taking care of the poor, the handicapped and the elderly? Which of the following possible reasons could explain it?
   - Koreans just got rich and haven't had enough time to set up welfare programs.
   - Koreans only care about themselves and their family, but not about other people.
9. Korea spends more on primary education than any other country in the world? Why do they spend so much on the very young but so little on the very old?
10. Which of these changes would you like to see occur in Korea?
    - Be more considerate of others, not just family members
    - Better driving habits, obey traffic laws
    - More open communication between employees and employers
    - Less pressure from society on how a person should behave, more freedom of expression

UNIT 20 The Educational Crisis

When Newsweek magazine printed a list of the world's top 100 universities in 2007 and not even one Korean university was on the list, it was a wake up call to Korean educators that something had to be done about the Korean educational system and soon.

The shock of not appearing on the list caused all of Korea's most respected universities domestically to make inclusion on the list next time around a top priority.

Seoul National University set a goal is to be in the top 30 by 2015 and in the top 10 by 2025. Yonsei's goal was even more ambitious than SNU's, planning to be in the top 10 by 2020, very lofty goals considering that neither had made even the list of the top 100. It wouldn't be an exaggeration to say that all of Korea's universities were suddenly feeling a sense of crisis.

Korean educators began to question the effectiveness of Korea's centralized educational system, which banned universities from giving their own entrance exams and banned high schools from being ranked.

By 2013 some progress had been made with two Korean universities making the list--Seoul National University at #41, and Korea Advanced Institute of Science and Technology (KAIST) at #73, but Korea's other top universities—Yonsei, Koryo, Sogang and Ehwa—were still not on the list. (see p.80)

Most top rankings went to US and UK schools.

Vocabulary

- **wake...call**: causing them to realize that something was wrong and had to be fixed
- **domestically**: pertaining to Korea only
- **next...around**: the next time they publish the list
- **ambitious**: not easily accomplished, requires a lot of effort
- **lofty**: very high
- **centralized**: all decision making in the hands of one central agency

Harvard still ranked No. 1 in the world.

In the wake of the shocking report issued by Newsweek, a number of foreign educators offered their advice as to what Korean universities should do to improve their standing worldwide. Some of them pointed out differences between Korea's system of education and those in the west.

One big difference is that Korea's educational system is highly centralized, with all decisions, rules, and regulations coming out of the Ministry of Education and Human Resources. Individual schools are given no authority to set their own higher standards if they want to, as they are in western countries. Most foreign educators see the lack of autonomy as a huge obstacle to the improvement of Korea's educational standards.

The western thinking toward educational excellence is that each school should determine what is best for its students and faculty and set goals accordingly. All foreign observers agree that setting goals according to a magazine ranking is the wrong way to go about improving the quality of education.

Some of the problems associated with Korea's educational system might explain why so many Koreans are bypassing Korea's educational system and studying abroad instead. If asked, every one of them will say that the standards are much higher overseas than in Korea.

In 2011 there were 73,000 Korean students in US universities, 30,000 in Australia, and another 8,000 in Canada. Korean students studying abroad are outnumbered only by students from China and India—2 countries with enormous populations.

Koreans studying abroad

Vocabulary

- **wake**: aftermath, the period after something happens
- **standing**: ranking, position
- **authority**: right, ability, power
- **autonomy**: independence, ability to decide for themselves what is best
- **educational excellence**: the best that can be achieved
- **to bypass**: to avoid it altogether (to pass it by)
- **standards**: amount of knowledge required to get a passing grade

Probably the best evidence of what's wrong with Korean education are the observations of educators who have taught overseas before teaching in Korea. The first thing most of them will mention is a lack of seriousness on the part of the students.

Korea's college entrance exam creates a feeling among students that after they get into the school of their choice, the battle is over. Students assume that once admitted, graduation will be a breeze. That's hardly the case with western universities, where being accepted is no guarantee of graduation.

The flunk-out rate at large universities in the US, Australia, or Canada can be as high as 30%. In the UK 20% flunk out the first year. That shows that students there have to work hard in order to stay in school.

Not so in the case in Korean universities, where Korean professors are often accused by foreign teachers of being too lenient with the students. Some Korean professors have been accused of "spoon feeding" students when they should be making them work harder.

Cheating on exams is commonplace at some schools, and foreign professors who fail students for cheating on tests are sometimes overruled by department heads who change the failing grades to C's.

"...professors who fail students are sometimes overruled by department heads who change the F's to C's."

Ironically, Korean high school education is considered among the best in the world with Koreans studying abroad ranking at the top on science and math tests, high enough to win the praise of US President Obama.

Being accepted into a US university is no guarantee of being able to graduate.

Lifestyle

Vocabulary

- **observations**: opinions based on their experiences
- **the...over**: they've already reached their goal, don't have to try hard anymore
- **be a breeze**: be very easy, nothing to worry about
- **flunk-out rate**: percentage of students who have to quit school due to failing grades
- **(be) lenient**: give them good grades without doing much study
- **(be) overruled**: reverse (cancel) the professor's decision
- **ironic**: get failing grades on tests

Top Global Universities by Reputation—2013*

1. Harvard University (US)
2. Massachusetts Institute of Technology (US)
3. University of Cambridge (UK)
4. University of Oxford (UK)
5. University of California, Berkeley (US)
6. Stanford University (US)
7. Princeton University (US)
8. University of California, Los Angeles (US)
9. University of Tokyo (Japan)
10. Yale University (US)
11. California Institute of Technology (US)
12. University of Michigan (US)
13. Columbia University (US)
14. University of Chicago (US)
15. Imperial College London (UK)
16. University of Toronto (Canada)
17. Cornell University (US)
18. University of Pennsylvania (US)
19. Johns Hopkins University (US)
20. University College London (UK)
21. Swiss Federal Institute. of Technology (ZH)
22. National University of Singapore (SG)
23. Kyoto University (Japan)
24. University of Illinois at Urbana (US)
25. London School of Economics (UK)
26. Carnegie Mellon University (US)
27. University of Washington (US)
28. New York University (US)
29. University of Texas at Austin (US)
30. University of Wisconsin-Madison (US)
31. University of British Colombia (Canada)
32. Duke University (US)
33. McGill University (Canada)
34. University of California San Diego (US)
35. Tsinghua University (China)
36. University of Hong Kong (Hong Kong)
37. Northwestern University (US)
38. Georgia Institute of Technology (US)
39. University of Melbourne (AU)
40. University of California San Francisco (US)
41. Seoul National University (Korea)
42. Australian National University (AU)
43. University of Massachusetts (US)
44. Ludwig-Maximilians Universitat Muchen (Ger.)
45. Peking University (China)
46. University of Edinburgh (UK)
47. University of Manchester (UK)
48. University of California Davis (US)
49. University of Sydney (AU)
50. Purdue University (US)
51. Delft University of Technology (Netherlands)
52. Ecole Polytechnique Fed. de Lausanne (CH)
53. Middle East Technical University (Turkey)
54. University of Minnesota (US)
55. University of N.C. at Chapel Hill (US)
56. Ohio University (US)
57. Osaka University (Japan)
58. Pennsylvania State University (US)
59. National Taiwan University (Taiwan)
73. Korea Adv. Inst. of Science and Tech. (Korea)

*Times Higher Education (www.timeshighereducation.co.uk)

DISCUSS

1. How can it be that Korea's high school education can be good enough to win the admiration of the world while its university education is ranked near the bottom? What's the reason for this?
2. What do you think of the fact that only two Korean universities made 2013's list of top 100 universities in the world? Tell why you think so.
   - It shows that there is something wrong with Korea's educational system.
   - It shows that there is something wrong with the ranking system.
   - It's better than 2007, so it shows that things are at least getting better.
3. What is your personal reaction to the news? How does it make you feel? Tell why.
   - I am embarrassed and ashamed.
   - It makes me angry.
   - It makes me feel that improving Korea's educational system must be a top priority.
4. Do you agree that Korean professors may be too lenient with the students? How would you describe the educational standards at your college or university? Do students have to work hard? Is the library busy all the time or just before exams?
5. Do you agree that most Korean students consider the entrance exam the hard part, and then after that, graduation is easy? Is that how you feel too? Why or why not?
6. Since there are 100,000 Korean students studying in just the US, Canada and Australia alone, what does that tell you about Korea's educational system? Tell why you think so.
   - It shows that the educational system in those countries is better.
   - It shows that there are a lot of rich Koreans who just want to get a foreign degree.
   - It shows that Korean universities have to improve a lot.
7. Almost all foreign educators say that Korea's educational system will have to be decentralized before it can be improved. In other words, the Ministry of Education will have to give universities the freedom to set their own standards. Do you think it will ever happen? Would you like to see it happen? Why or why not?
8. The flunk-out rate at Korea's universities is very low compared to in foreign countries. Would you like to see Korean universities start to flunk out more students? Why or why not?

UNIT 21 International Sports

Celebrating Incheon's selection as host of the 2014 Asian Games.

For Korean athletes one day in April of 2007 was déjà vu and cause for jubilation all over again. For the 5th time in a little over 2 decades Korea was once again chosen as the site of an international sports competition. Incheon had just been chosen to host the biggest sports competition in Asia—the 2014 Asian Games.

Korea was first put on the international sports map when Seoul and Pusan hosted the 1986 Asian Games. That was followed by the 1988 Seoul Olympics just two years later. Koreans were ecstatic because their formerly war-torn country had been put on the map for some other reason than the Korean War and border clashes on its northern border. For the first time in history tourists were no longer afraid to come to Korea. The Korean tourist industry was born.

Korea's third and fourth appearances on the international sports calendar were in 2002 when Korea shared hosting the World Cup with Japan and then the Asian Games in Pusan.

> "Incheon already had 11 Olympic-standard stadiums, much better infrastructure, and more money."

Incheon competed against New Delhi, India for the 2014 Asiad, but Incheon easily won the bid. The city already had 11 Olympic standard sports facilities, much better infrastructure, and more money. All three factors combined to make the selection of Incheon almost a slam dunk.

Vocabulary

Well-developed infrastructure

- **cause...jubilation**: reason to be very happy
- **ecstatic**: extremely excited and happy
- **put...map**: became famous, well-known
- **clashes**: conflicts, arguments
- **bid**: request to be allowed to host the games
- **infrastructure**: transportation, hotel accommodations, communications network, etc.
- **slam dunk**: a slang expression meaning something certain to happen

Both the city of Incheon and all of Korea had good reason to be excited about being chosen to host yet another major international sporting event. For decades the country was frustrated in trying to make the world realize that there was much more to Korea than just the Korean war and its standoff with the North.

Koreans in Kuwait celebrating the decision.

When Incheon was chosen to host the fifth major sporting event in a quarter century it proved that Korea's image as a poor war ravaged country really had been put to rest.

Another reason to be jubilant was the economic impact the games would have on Incheon and on the whole country. At least 270,000 jobs had to be created in order to prepare for the Games.

Seventeen new sports facilities needed to be built, and four existing facilities had to be upgraded. New aquatics and tennis complexes would have to be built.

Economically, the news couldn't have come at a better time, since Korean business was in a slump and unemployment was high.

> "Economically, the news couldn't have come at a better time."

Korea loves hosting mega-sports events so much that it can't get enough. In 2013 it submitted a bid to host the 2020 Summer Olympics along with its co-host for the 2002 World Cup—arch-rival Japan.

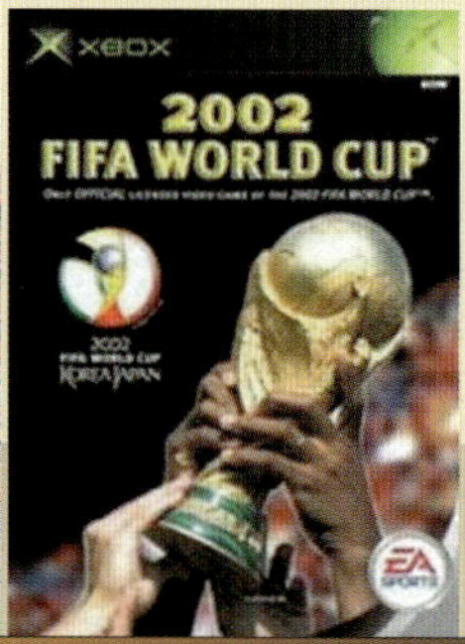

Another great sports moment for Korea: The 2002 FIFA World Cup

Vocabulary

- **had...to**: a good reason
- **frustrated**: trying hard but not succeeding
- **standoff...North**: conflict with North Korea
- **(be) put to rest**: no longer valid, no longer something that people think of
- **impact**: effect
- **(be) upgraded**: made more modern, fixed
- **aquatics**: swimming pools for water sports
- **slump**: period of bad economic times

Memorable moments in Korean International games hosting

Final Positions

Champions	Brazil
Runners-up	Germany
Third Place	Turkey
Fourth Place	South Korea

Korea came in 4th in the 2002 World Cup

Taekwondo demo at the '88 Seoul Olympics opening ceremony

Ahn Jung Hwan's goal results in a 1-1 draw with the USA.

1988 Seoul Olympics opening ceremony.

Red Shirt supporters during the 2002 World Cup in Korea.

Red Shirt fan.

Spectacular closing ceremony of the ´02 Busan Asian Games.

WORD PRACTICE

Fill in the correct word.

1. Incheon won the bid for the 2014 Asiad because of its better____.
2. The selection of Incheon was practically a____dunk.
3. Koreans were____that foreigners all associated Korea with war.
4. They wanted to put that perception to____.
5. Koreans were____that Korea was put on the____for a good reason.
6. Hosting an big sports event has a big____on the Korean economy.
7. Some sports facilities had to be____in order to host the events.
8. Korea co-hosted the 2002 World Cup with____Japan.
9. The____World Cup closing ceremony was held in Busan.

a. rest
b. slam
c. arch-rival
d. upgraded
e. ecstatic
f. frustrated
g. spectacular
h. impact
i. map
j. infrastructure

Answers on page 160.

DISCUSS

1. How important is it for Korea to host international sports events? What is to be gained by it? Tell why you think so.
2. Korea hosted the Asian Games in 1986 and 2002 and the World Cup in 2002, but the last time India hosted the games was in 1982. Don't you think it would have been better to give the 2014 games to India instead of Korea? Isn't Korea getting too much at the expense of other countries? Tell why you think so.
3. What do you think is the most important aspect of Incheon's being awarded the honor of hosting the 2014 Asian Games? Consider each of the following.
   - International prestige—the world's attention focused on Korea
   - Economic—all the money that Korea will make from the foreign investment and visitors
   - Athletics—Korean athletes having a chance to perform before a friendly, home crowd
   - Diplomatic—the chance for Korea to improve its relationships with foreign countries
   - Employment situation—the many jobs that will be created for Koreans
4. How much of an effect will the 2014 Asiad have on Incheon's dream of becoming the business hub of Asia? Will it have a major effect or will the effect be very small? Tell why you think so.
5. How much of an effect will having the Games in Korea have on Korean athletes? Will they perform better at home than if they were in a foreign country? Will they win more medals? Tell why you think so.
6. Korea has been the site of many more international sporting events than Japan. Do you think the Japanese people are angry about that? What if the situation were reversed and Japan was doing the hosting? Would Korea be angry? Why or why not?
7. How does North Korea feel about the fact that South Korea continues to host prestigious sporting events like the World Cup and the Asian Games? Does it make them jealous or angry? Tell why you think so?

8. Would you like to see North Korea co-host the 2014 Asian Games, or should all the events be held in South Korea? Does North Korea have enough money to build facilities to host any events?
9. Back in the 1980s Korea had to fight off its image as a war-torn country. What is the image most foreigners have in their minds today when they think of Korea? How has the world's perception of South Korea changed?

UNIT 22 The Employment Crisis

Employment prospects for today's college students have never been more dismal. Even worse, the chance of things getting any better in the foreseeable future is approximately zero. Everybody knows what the situation is, and it's hard to find a student who isn't worried sick about finding a job after graduation.

> "It seems that Koreans are too well educated for their own good."

To begin with, there are too many college graduates for the number of white collar jobs available. It seems that Koreans are too well educated for their own good. The number of students entering college increased from 130,000 in 1990 to 330,000 in 2006.

At the same time, the number of professional jobs available shrank by 80,000 because of an economic recession that forced businesses to cut back on hiring. The result is a glut of college graduates like Korea has never seen before.

The oversupply of college-educated people has the potential of turning into a huge crisis for Korean society. To illustrate how serious the problem is, 150,000 people applied for just 900 government jobs in the fall of 2006.

In April of 2007 the Korea Times published an article that would probably not have been printed a decade earlier. The article was titled, "Reasons Not Everybody Needs to Go to Elite College", an attempt to make Koreans realize that some people are just not cut out for a high quality education.

Should every Korean child go to college?

Vocabulary

- **dismal**: very depressing
- **the...zero**: almost no possibility that the situation will improve soon
- **(be) worried sick**: be extremely worried
- **for...good**: problems created because they are too well educated
- **shrank**: decreased
- **glut**: oversupply, more than what is needed
- **(be) cut out for**: not be suitable for

Most Korean college grads would rather die than take a job as a store clerk.

The unemployment rate for people in their 20s is more than 15% if the ones who have given up looking for work are included. This high number of unemployed is turning many young people into hermits, still living at home and with nowhere to go. The Dongnam Psychiatric Clinic estimated that there were between 30,000 and 40,000 of them in 2005. Some of them have already committed suicide.

The irony of this situation is that while thousands of college grads sit unemployed at home, 200,000 positions sit vacant at small and medium-sized businesses. The labor shortage at these businesses is so severe that some of them are having trouble staying in business. Their employees are overworked, and their productivity is hurt.

> "The high number of unemployed is turning many young people into hermits, still living at home with nowhere to go."

In almost any other country except Korea, the two problems would cancel each other out. In the west, when people can't find jobs in their own fields, they usually take whatever jobs they can get. But if Koreans can't find jobs in their own fields of study, they'd rather sit at home than do a job they consider beneath their dignity.

Lee Jae Chan, 47, grandson of Samsung founder Lee Byung Chul, committed suicide in 2010 after being unemployed for 10 years.

Vocabulary

- **given...work**: they stopped looking for a job
- **turning...hermits**: making them stay in the house without going out at all
- **(be) living at home**: living with their parents
- **sit vacant**: are available, in need of somebody to do the job
- **staying...business**: keep from going bankrupt
- **productivity**: the amount of goods or services that they can produce
- **cancel...out**: the second problem would solve the first problem
- **beneath...dignity**: not good enough for their position in society

To say that Koreans are lazy because they won't take jobs below their level of education would be an oversimplification of the situation. It really has a lot to do with "saving face". Korean culture places a lot of emphasis on one's position in society. In Korea it really matters what kind of a house a person lives in, what kind of car he drives, and most of all, what kind of job he has.

> "In Korea it really matters what kind of house a person lives in, [and] what kind of car he drives."

Some unemployed college grads have been known to dress up and leave the house each morning, then come back at night, just so the neighbors will think they have good jobs.

An unemployed college grad in a western country might take a job as a taxi driver or a construction worker if that's the only kind of job he could find, but such a thing is inconceivable in Korea. Even an office job with a small, unknown company would be unthinkable, even if the job paid well.

Korean college grads won't do construction jobs

What's the solution to Korea's employment crisis of college grads sitting around unemployed while blue collar industries can't fill their job vacancies.

The only possible solution is for Koreans to change their way of thinking. That may be asking a lot, but there is no other way. Either college grads start accepting jobs beneath their dignity or a lot of small and medium- sized businesses will go bust.

This UK jobs site for college grads has information on getting jobs as taxi drivers.

Vocabulary

- **oversimplification**: not as simple as that
- **to dress up**: put on business clothes, e.g., a suit and a tie
- **(be) inconceivable**: something that can't even be imagined, totally impossible
- **the...well**: salary or wages very high
- **(be) asking...lot**: maybe more than they are capable of doing
- **go bust**: go bankrupt, have to close up business

WORD PRACTICE

Fill in the correct word.

1. Many college students are worried____about finding a good job.
2. Employment prospects for today's students are truly____.
3. The problem is that there is now a____of college grads.
4. Koreans may be too well education for their own____.
5. The unemployment crisis is turning many college grads into____.
6. Jobs at small businesses sit____while many grads are____.
7. It's____that a Korean college grad would take a job as a taxi driver.
8. They won't do jobs that they consider____their dignity.
9. Maybe not everyone is____out for a college education.

a. sick
b. glut
c. beneath
d. cut
e. good
f. unemployed
g. inconceivable
h. dismal
i. vacant
j. hermits

Answers on page 160.

DISCUSS

Lifestyle

1. How long will it take before some of the unemployed college grads decide to start taking some of the vacant positions at small and medium-sized companies? Tell why you think so.
   - Very soon. It's already happening.
   - When their parents stop giving them money.
   - Never. Graduates of top universities will never work for no-name companies.
2. The biggest problem is that there are too many college grads in Korea to fill the limited number of white collar (professional) jobs, and not enough people who don't have college educations. Should some high school students be discouraged from going to college? why or why not?
3. The number of high school students getting into college increased 3 times between 1990 and 2006. How can that happen? Tell why you think so.
   - Korean universities are accepting more students in order to make more money.
   - Today's high school students are 3 times smarter than the students in 1990.
4. What would be the best way to reduce the number of college graduates, which would have the effect of fewer college grads looking for jobs?
   - Universities should make it harder to be admitted.
   - Universities should flunk out more students.
   - Close down some of the universities. There are too many universities in Korea.
5. About 86% of Korean high school students go to college, compared to just 42% in the USA. Is it reasonable to think that every college grad will find an executive position? Shouldn't the college enrollment rate be cut?
6. If small and medium-sized businesses start to go bankrupt because they can't find enough workers, will unemployed college grads take those jobs? Why or why not?
7. What do you think about the fact that college students in western countries will do any kind of job, even drive a taxi, if they can't find a professional job? Tell why you think so.
   - I think it's great. Koreans should do the same.
   - They're stupid. College grads should never do low-class jobs.
8. There is an oversupply of college grads in Korea. The Korean government wants to discourage high school students from going to college. Do you agree with this line of thinking?

A college entrance cram school

9. If you have children of your own, will you insist that they go to college? Why or why not?

UNIT 23

Outdoor Advertising

Koreans live in a world of signs and advertisements. It's one of the first things visitors to the country notice: signs are everywhere. There is no escape. There are ads on billboards beside highways or mounted high on city buildings, many of them animated, on subway station walls, inside subway cars and buses, on TV and on Internet websites.

Of course, the same thing could be said of just about every other country in the world where people have money to spend, but Korea has something most other countries don't have—"sign buildings". These are buildings that are so completely covered with signs that a person has to look very hard to find the doors and windows. In most cases, the windows are also covered with signs. Instead of putting all business names on a signboard, as they do in other countries (see picture below), they plaster the signs all over the building itself.

These buildings are actually mini-malls that serve the people who live in apartment towns. A typical sign building would have a mini supermarket, a dry cleaner/laundry, a greengrocer, a bakery, a hair dresser, maybe even a language institute for children. Most Koreans think that sign buildings are eyesores.

A Korean shopping mall signboard in Las Vegas

Vocabulary

- **(be) mounted**: placed, positioned
- **(be) animated**: moving pictures created by moving lights
- **could...of**: it is also true of...
- **to plaster**: to cover something with, put it all over
- **greengrocer**: a store where fruits and vegetables are sold
- **eyesores**: things unpleasant to look at, ugly

Highway billboards were banned until 1985.

Back in the days before Korea became the affluent society that it is today, Korean roadsides were among the most scenic in Asia. Japanese visitors to Korea <u>marveled at</u> the <u>unmarred</u> beauty of the Korean countryside, since their own rural areas were <u>littered with</u> billboards and signs.

"Japanese visitors to Korea marveled at the unmarred beauty of the Korean countryside."

But that was then and this is now. As the number of cars increased, the number of billboards along the roads also increased. It's now hard to take a picture of the countryside without getting a billboard or two in <u>the shot</u>.

In 2001 the Korean government decided to do something about it. They forced the owners of illegal billboards to take them down. They counted almost 56,000 illegal advertisements on the 673 km. of 6-lane highways just around Seoul.

One type of outdoor advertisement that people don't mind are the animated <u>LED</u> screens that can be found in subway and train stations, in bus terminals, inside trains or mounted high on downtown office buildings. Huge LED screens are positioned so that drivers can watch them while waiting at traffic lights.

While they are exciting and eye-catching, they can also be very distracting to <u>someone behind the wheel</u>. Many accidents have been caused by drivers who were too busy watching the action on animated LED screens.

Can cause traffic accidents

Vocabulary

- **to marvel (at)**: be amazed at
- **unmarred**: unspoiled, not ruined, perfect
- **(be) littered with**: covered with...(something not good, like garbage)
- **the shot**: the picture (comes from snapshot)
- **LED**: stands for "Light Emitting Diode" (uses much less electricity than LCD)
- **someone...wheel**: somebody driving a car

Foreigners love it, Koreans don't.

There is some disagreement over the display of neon lights that fill the entertainment areas of every city in Korea. Most foreigners think the hangul sign alleys are exciting and exotic, but more Koreans think they look cluttered.

To many Koreans these sign-filled streets and pedestrian alleyways are just more examples of the Korean habit of plastering buildings with signs. Sometimes the problem is that, while undeniably eye-catching, the signs seem to be competing with one another for the viewer's attention, resulting in an overdose of color. It's a case of too much of a good thing, at which point what starts out as attractive becomes an eyesore.

"Some of the ads on subway walls show nudity and sexually-suggestive poses."

Until recently Korean billboard ads were much less provocative than the ones in western countries, but that really isn't true anymore. Some of the ads on subway walls show nudity and sexually-suggestive poses. Many Koreans think that the new ads cross the line. They worry that they may soon look like the ones in western countries, which are even worse.

Sexually suggestive advertising in Seoul..

...and in New York.

Vocabulary

- **exotic**: unfamiliar and exciting (NOT the same as *erotic*, which means sexy)
- **cluttered**: too many items squeezed together
- **pedestrian alleyways**: very narrow side streets suitable only for people walking
- **overdose**: too much of something, more than a proper amount
- **too...thing**: when there's too much of it, then it's not good anymore.
- **provocative**: in the case of advertising, usually means suggesting sex
- **cross the line**: beyond what is acceptable, beyond the limit of good taste

WORD PRACTICE

Fill in the correct word.

1. Some billboards are____high on tall buildings.
2. Sign buildings are____with the names of businesses.
3. Most Koreans consider the sign buildings as____.
4. The Japanese countryside was____with billboards and signs.
5. Visitors____at the____beauty of the Korean countryside.
6. Foreigners think the colorful hangul signboards look____,
7. Some of the new advertisements are as____as western ones.
8. Too many signs in the same place make the scene too____.
9. The question is whether the signs____the line of decency.

a. littered
b. plastered
c. cross
d. exotic
e. unmarred
f. provocative
g. mounted
h. cluttered
i. marveled
j. eyesores

Answers on page 160.

DISCUSS

1. Do you agree that there is too much outside advertising in Korea? If so, where do you especially find advertisements annoying?
2. Should there be laws to ban advertisements from certain places? If so, where would you like to see advertising restricted?

Distracting to drivers?

3. What do you think about billboard advertising along Korean roads and highways? Do they distract drivers, or keep them awake? Tell why you think so.
4. Why do Korean businesses put their ads all over "sign buildings" instead of on large signposts (page 85) as they do in most western countries? What do you think of the sign buildings—attractive, unattractive, or doesn't matter?
5. What do you think of Korean entertainment areas? Do you agree that they are attractive and colorful, or do you think they're too cluttered? Would you call them beautiful or ugly?
6. The walls inside subway stations are plastered with huge advertisements. Do you find those advertisements attractive or are they an eyesore?
7. What type of advertising are you the most influenced by and which type do you usually ignore? Which of the following do you think are the most *effective*, and which are probably *ignored* by most people and why?
   a. TV commercials.
   b. Ads on the Internet
   c. Ads inside subway stations and subway cars
   d. Huge animated LED screens mounted on office buildings
   e. Highway billboards

Underwear ad: crossing the line?

8. Do you think ads that show sex or nudity cross the line? Should advertisers be able to display whatever kind of ads they want? Would you like to see ads like this one in Korean subway stations? Why or why not?
9. What do you think of the little sticker ads that merchants put on apartment doors and inside elevators? Would you mind living in a building where the walls, elevators, and doors are plastered with sticker ads? Why or why not?
10. Are there any products that should be restricted from being advertised? How about cigarettes, alcohol, or condoms? Should they be advertised on TV? Why or why not?

UNIT 24

Korea & Climate Change

Asia in 2050?

Each year since 2000 average worldwide temperatures have been hotter than the year before. The hottest years ever recorded have all occurred since 1995. The arctic ice cap is melting. There's no doubt that the earth has entered a period of global warming.

As the world's 12th largest producer of CO_2, the greenhouse gas mostly responsible for the warming, Korea shares much of the blame for the problem. What happens in the world is important to Korea because extreme weather, which is caused by global warming, is already taking a heavy toll on the country.

One effect of global warming is a rise in sea level due to the melting of glaciers and ice near the north and south poles. Asia is especially vulnerable because many of its biggest cities are located by the sea and will surely be at least partially underwater.

"Asia is especially vulnerable... and will surely be at least partially underwater."

Korea is fortunate that most of its major cities are located inland, but all of the low lying coastal areas in the south and the west (see map) will be lost to the sea.

The black areas could all go underwater.

Environment

Vocabulary

- **(be) recorded**: statistics kept about it
- **CO_2**: carbon dioxide, the waste product of burning oil, gas and coal
- **greenhouse gas**: traps the sun's heat inside the atmosphere like a greenhouse
- **extreme weather**: weather that causes a lot of damage
- **taking a toll**: already causing damage
- **glaciers**: large areas of ice covering land.
- **vulnerable**: can easily be affected

Typhoon Rusa (2002)

Koreans are very concerned about what effects global warming could have on their country. In a survey taken by a Canadian environmental opinion survey group in 2005, 77% of Koreans said they were very worried. Among the 30 countries surveyed, Koreans ranked No. 4 among those worried the most, and it's no wonder.

"Among 30 countries surveyed, Koreans ranked No. 4 among those worried the most."

The summer of 1998 brought a devastating flood. Korea experienced the worst drought in 100 years in 2001, the same year that the average global temperature was 1℃. higher than normal.

Just one year later, in 2002, those same parched fields were submerged in flood waters caused by Typhoon Rusa, the worst typhoon in 43 years. In 2006 ten people were drowned by another flood. In 2013 Japan and Korea recorded the hottest temperatures on record with some nighttime temperatures falling only to 31 degrees Celsius.

Han River flood (2006)

More snow fell in one month in 2004 than in any other year since record keeping began 100 years earlier. Koreans sense that something strange is happening to their weather, and they're right.

Koreans trying to cool off in 2013

Environment

Vocabulary

- **(be) no wonder**: not surprising, to be expected
- **devastating**: causing much destruction, damage
- **parched**: thirsty, extremely dry, in need of water
- **submerged**: covered by water
- **on record**: ever recorded by the weather bureau.
- **sense**: feel (have the sensation that)

Koreans say they are worried about global warming, but are they willing to do anything about it? As one of the world's biggest emitters of greenhouse gases, Korea not only has the power to make a difference but also has an obligation to the world to do so.

However, at the rate that Korea's energy consumption is increasing, it would seem that the answer to the above question is "no". While claiming to be worried about global warming, Koreans have been producing CO_2 like there's no tomorrow.

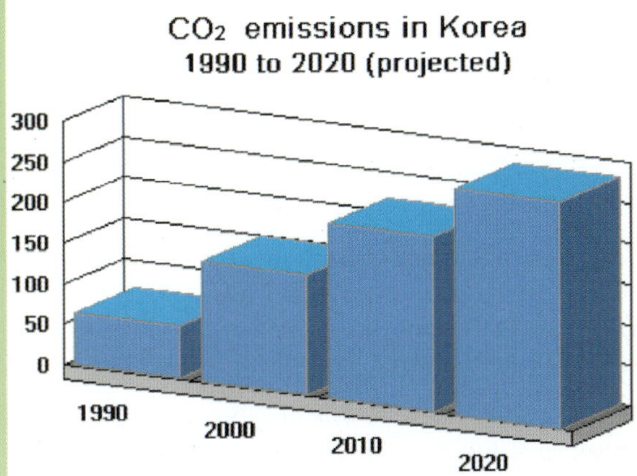

Air pollution in Korea has reached a crisis level because of the country's love affair with the automobile. But Koreans seem willing to sacrifice the environment in order to drive big cars that burn diesel fuel. Diesel fuel is 15% more energy efficient than gasoline, but it's also 15% dirtier than gasoline. Diesel fuel has helped turn Seoul's deep blue sky of the 1980s into the hazy gray sky that it has become.

"Koreans have been producing CO_2 like there's no tomorrow."

Global warming isn't a problem that Korea can solve alone, but Koreans can and should help. Unless they're willing to make some big lifestyle changes to reduce their use of energy, they will only guarantee that the extreme weather they are so worried about will just get worse.

Seoul before cars and now.
What happened to the blue sky?

Environment

Vocabulary

- **emitters**: countries that release CO_2 into the atmosphere
- **make a difference**: take some action that will improve the situation
- **energy consumption**: the amount of oil, gas, and coal they use per year
- **like...tomorrow**: they think only about now, like they don't care about the future
- **crisis level**: at an extremely harmful degree
- **energy efficient**: use less energy, produce less CO2
- **hazy**: not clear, can't see far away because of all the dirt in the air

WORD PRACTICE

Fill in the correct word.

1. The hottest years ever____have all been since 1995.
2. CO_2 is the____gas most responsible for____warming.
3. Asian cities are very____to the rise of sea level.
4. Korea experienced a____typhoon named Rusa in 2002.
5. Fields were____in flood waters.
6. Koreans____that something is happening to their weather.
7. 2013 was the hottest summer on____in Korea and Japan.
8. Koreans produce CO_2 gas like there's no____.
9. Korea is at a____level because of their love of automobiles.

a. greenhouse
b. tomorrow
c. submerged
d. devastating
e. crisis
f. recorded
g. record
h. sense
i. global
j. vulnerable

Answers on page 160.

DISCUSS

1. What do you think about global warming? It is really happening, or is the earth just going through a natural warming period? Tell why you think so.
2. How serious is the problem of global warming for Korea? Tell why you think so.
   a. Very serious. Korea will be affected a lot by it.
   b. A little serious. Most of the effects will take place outside of Korea.
   c. Not serious. Korea has nothing to worry about.
3. When asked about it 77% of Koreans said they were very worried about global warming, but they are continuing to produce more greenhouse gases. How can they do that if they are really worried about global warming? Which statement is the truth?
   a. Koreans say that they're worried, but they're not really very worried.
   b. Most Koreans don't realize that burning more oil hurts the environment.
   c. Koreans are lazy. They want other countries to solve the problem.
4. Since Korea is the 12th largest emitter of CO_2, how much responsibility does Korea have in trying to stop the global warming? Tell why you think so.
   a. Same as the top 11%.
   b. Much less than the biggest polluters
   c. The same as every other country in the world.
5. Since diesel fuel is 15% dirtier than gasoline do should car companies stop selling cars that run on diesel? Why or why not?
6. In most other countries diesel fuel is more expensive than gasoline, but in Korea diesel is cheaper. Which is better—cheaper gas or cheaper diesel? Tell why you think so.
7. Will Koreans ever give up their love of big automobiles in favor of small cars that produce less CO_2? Why or why not?

Global warming did this to the Arctic ice sheet in just 32 years.

8. What would have to happen for Koreans to get serious about reducing their energy consumption—a huge typhoon? Several years of drought? Rising sea level? Or will Koreans never do anything at all about it, no matter what happens? Tell why you think so.
9. Will the world change its ways and stop global warming, or will global warming ruin life as we know it, just as predicted? Tell why you think so.

Environment

UNIT 25

Driving in Korea

Driving home for Chuseok

When it comes to driving in Korea, following the old saying, "When in Rome, do as the Romans do" could cost you your life. Saying that driving in Korea is a little dangerous would be putting it mildly. One foreigner riding a bus counted 47 red lights on his journey and said that the bus stopped for just 3 of them. People who are brave enough to drive on Korean roads on a regular basis really do take their lives into their own hands.

Twenty-one people die on Korean roads every day. According to the Road Traffic Safety Authority (RTSA), 60% of accidents are caused by reckless driving. In other words, 13 lives could be saved every day if people would just drive more safely. That's 4,745 people per year who would still be alive instead of dead.

Obviously, Korean drivers do many things wrong, such as drive too fast and ignore traffic laws, but the main causes of accidents are impatience and the refusal to yield the right of way. Nobody wants to let anybody else get ahead, so two drivers make a dash for the same space at the same time, resulting in a crash.

"Bus drivers are particularly guilty of driving through red lights..."

Korean drivers also hate to wait for red lights, so sometimes, when they think there aren't any policemen around, they'll just drive through. Bus drivers are particularly guilty of this, thinking that their tight schedules give them special permission to ignore traffic laws.

Speeding kills.

Vocabulary

- **cost...life**: you might get killed
- **putting...mildly**: an understatement, in fact, it's much more than just "a little"
- **take...hands**: take a chance that they might get injured or killed
- **impatience**: refusing to wait
- **yield...way**: letting another driver go first
- **make...dash**: driving very fast (to prevent someone else getting there first)
- **tight schedules...laws**: think that they are too busy to stop and wait for red lights

Environment

A big part of the problem with driving in Korea is that many Korean drivers don't see it as a problem. Foreigners who complain about the bad driving are usually told that they just don't understand Korean culture.

The first problem with that line of thinking is that Koreans who return home after living abroad are among the loudest to complain. After experiencing more orderly driving in western countries they are appalled by the chaos they find on Korean roads.

Running a red light

The other problem is that statistics don't lie. Korea has one of the highest traffic accident rates in the world. What this shows is that understanding Korean society doesn't have anything to do with it.

Traffic accidents are the number one cause of deaths among Koreans under the age of 30. In 2003 there were 240,832 accidents resulting in 376,503 injuries and 7,212 deaths. That works out to 660 accidents, 1,031 injuries and 21 deaths per day on Korean roads.

A familiar sight—chalk marks where accidents occurred

But there is good news to report. Today's accident rate is 40% lower than it was in the early 1990s. In those years there were over 14,000 traffic accidents in Korea per year. That's 14,000 for 75% fewer cars than today. So compared to then, driving in Korea today is almost a paradise.

> "Foreigners who complain about the bad driving are told that they don't understand Korean culture."

Which driver ran the red light?

Eating while driving

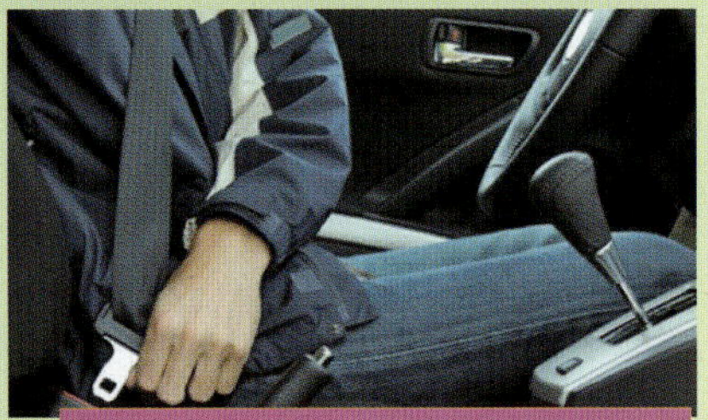

Not using a seat belt costs many lives in Korea.

Vocabulary

- **don't...as**: don't think that it is...
- **(be) appalled (by)**: be shocked, horrified
- **chaos**: complete lack of order
- **run...light**: not stopping when the light turns red
- **work...to**: calculates to

It's not hard to understand why Korea has one of the worst traffic accident records in the world. According to the RTSA, the most common reasons for accidents, deaths and injuries are

- Running red lights
- Tailgating
- Refusing to yield the right of way
- Ignoring lane markings
- Drunk driving
- Talking on cell phones
- Refusal to use safety belts
- Speeding

Korean police have a hard time trying to control the situation. They've tried everything from policemen dummies to hidden cameras to crackdowns, but nothing seems to work. Drivers figure out where the dummies are and then just ignore them. They memorize where the cameras are hidden, so they slow down before they get to them and speed up again as soon as they pass.

Police crackdowns haven't been very effective either because drivers drive more safely while the crackdowns are ongoing and then go back to their reckless driving habits as soon as the crackdowns end. The police don't help the situation by announcing the dates of the crackdowns because then everybody knows when the crackdowns are going to start and when they'll end.

Ignoring lane markings

It has been suggested by both foreign traffic analysts and Koreans themselves that the real reason for the reckless driving is Korean impatience.

But in all fairness, not ALL Koreans are bad drivers. Women are among the best drivers in the country, and there are many safe men drivers too. It is a case where the saying "One bad apple spoils the barrel" fits, except that there are too many bad apples.

Using a cell phone while driving

Environment

Vocabulary

- **Tailgating**: driving too close to the car in front
- **Speeding**: driving faster than the speed limit
- **dummies**: plastic dolls that look like humans
- **crackdowns**: when police check more carefully than usual
- **(be) ongoing**: be in progress
- **traffic analysts**: experts who study traffic problems
- **One...barrel**: the bad drivers makes the situation bad for everybody

Speeding

WORD PRACTICE

Fill in the correct word.

1. Saying that driving in Korea is dangerous is putting it____.
2. When you get behind the____you take your____into your hands.
3. Most accidents in Korea are probably caused by____.
4. Koreans returning from abroad are____at the____on Korean roads.
5. Many accidents are caused by drivers who____red lights.
6. Following behind another car too close is called____.
7. Police____don't seem to help very much.
8. ____policemen are good for making drivers slow down.

a. mildly
b. impatience
c. appalled
d. run
e. life
f. chaos
g. dummy
h. tailgating
i. crackdowns
j. wheel

Answers on page 160.

DISCUSS

1. Do you agree that driving in Korea is dangerous? Tell why you think so.
2. How do you think driving in Korea compares to driving in other countries? Tell why you think so.
   a. It's probably more dangerous in Korea.
   b. It's probably less dangerous than in other countries.
   c. It's probably just the same as in other countries.
3. What do you think explains the high traffic accident rate in Korea? Tell why you think so.
   a. Too many cars, not enough roads
   b. Poor driver education system
   c. Koreans are too impatient
   d. Too many drivers for the police to control
4. What do you think about efforts by the Korean police to stop the reckless driving? Give your opinion on each one of these methods.
   a. Dummy policemen
   b. Crackdowns on bad driving
   c. Hidden cameras

Dummy policeman and car

5. Do you think It's a good idea for the police to announce when crackdowns will start and when they will end? Why or why not?
   a. What do you think about paying citizens to take pictures of traffic violations and then sending the pictures to the police? Is that a good way to stop bad drivers?
6. Korea's traffic accident rate is much higher than in all industrialized countries. The Korean government thinks that the poor traffic safety record is an obstacle to Korea's becoming one of the advanced countries of the world. Do you agree? Why or why not?
7. During the months leading up to the 2002 FIFA World Cup traffic accidents in Korea fell by about 2,000 in the year 2001 alone. Why do you think that happened?
8. Traffic accidents have decreased a lot since the 1990s. Why do you think that happened?
9. Traffic accidents have been on the decline since 2000. Why do you think that is? Which is getter better?
   a. driving habits
   b. the roads and highways
   c. traffic enforcement (policemen)
   d. driver education

UNIT 26 Preserving the DMZ

It's hard to believe that anything good could have come out of the devastating war between the North and the South that occurred between 1950 and 1953, but something did. It turns out that the DMZ, the uninhabited 4-km. wide strip of land that has separated the two bitter enemies for more than half a century is now one of the earth's few remaining natural refuges for many species of rare birds, animals and plants. Who could have imagined that anything so good could come out of the ravages of war?

"Who could have imagined that anything so good could come out of the ravages of war?"

Destroyed by bombs and land mine explosions, the DMZ has remained untouched by humans for 60 years while nature reclaimed it for itself. It is now a sanctuary for some animals and plants seen nowhere else on the Korean peninsula. The DMZ exists as the last remnant of Korea's natural state, going back thousands of years. It is what the Korean peninsula would be like if the 70 million people who now inhabit it didn't live there.

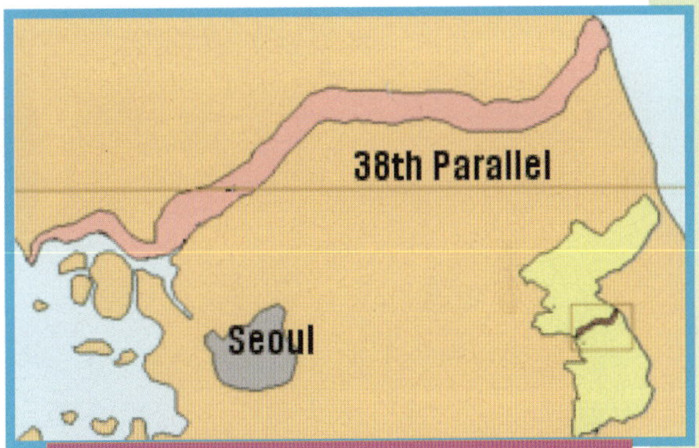

The DMZ: one of the last natural refuges.

Environment

Vocabulary

- **devastating**: destructive, caused much damage
- **uninhabited**: without human habitation, nobody lives there
- **natural refuge**: area where only animals can live, humans cannot enter
- **ravages**: death and destruction
- **reclaimed**: took back what it was originally its own
- **sanctuary**: safe place
- **remnant**: remaining part, left over from the past
- **if...there**: if no people lived there, if it were uninhabited

Nobody ever thought of the DMZ as a natural refuge until relations between the North and South began to warm up in the mid-1990s. Suddenly people started to think about what was going to happen to the DMZ if the two sides reunited.

Environmentalists from all around the world were horrified at the thought of the DMZ being overrun by bulldozers making way for new apartments, roads, and gas stations. They immediately began to map out a strategy for protecting it. Not surprisingly, their goal is to see that the DMZ is transformed into a national wildlife refuge if and when the two Koreas finally settle their differences and reunite.

Although the DMZ is only 4 kilometers wide, it is 250 kilometers long. That means 1000 square kilometers of potential natural refuge for all the animals and plants living there, some of which are on the endangered list. Among the rare species of animals living there are the Siberian tiger, the Asiatic black bear, Amur leopards, and Chinese egrets, a type of bird.

> "Environmentalists...were horrified at the thought of the DMZ being overrun by bulldozers."

The idea that all of these rare creatures of nature could be forced to scramble for their lives in order to make room for more shopping malls and gas stations is too ghastly a scenario for environmentalists to imagine. If they have anything to say about it, it's never going to happen.

An environmentalist's dream: the DMZ Wildlife Preserve

a bulldozer

Vocabulary

- **Environmentalists**: people who care about the environment
- **bulldozers**: construction machinery that digs up and moves the land
- **map...strategy**: decide what they're going to do
- **wildlife**: animals and plants that live without the help of human beings
- **settle...differences**: come to an agreement, end their conflict
- **scramble...lives**: run away in fear of being killed
- **too...scenario**: a horrible possible result or situation
- **if...it**: if they have the power to decide

It isn't clear where the Korean public stands on the issue since reunification still seems to be some way off. Dialogue with North Korea has been an on-again, off-again affair for the past 2 decades.

But nobody doubts that someday, sooner or later, there will be some kind of settlement, and the question about what to do about the DMZ will be front page news.

Even though the public has yet to be polled on what they think, it's hoped that a majority of people would not want to chase away all the animals in order to build more strip malls or garbage dumps.

But no South Korean president after Kim Young Sam has made any commitment to preserving the natural state of the DMZ. The only leader besides Kim who ever showed any interest in saving the DMZ was deceased North Korean dictator, Kim Jong Il, who once called it "a worthy goal."

"The only leader [besides Kim Young Sam] who ever showed any interest in saving the DMZ was...King Jong Il."

In all, 51 species of animals that have been wiped out on the rest of the peninsula since the war still live in the protected natural paradise of the DMZ.

Strip malls in the DMZ?

Amur leopard and **Asiatic black bear**, 2 of the endangered species whose habitats would be destroyed.

Environment

Vocabulary

- **where...on**: what their opinion is, what they think about it
- **some...off**: not going to happen soon
- **an...affair**: sometimes talking, sometimes not talking
- **front...news**: an important issue that everybody is talking about
- **strip malls**: small shopping areas with several stores side by side
- **(be) wiped out**: be killed, eliminated forever
- **the rest of**: all other places (except for this one area)

WORD PRACTICE

Fill in the correct word.

1. The DMZ is an____strip of land between the two Koreas.
2. It is a natural____for many____species of animals.
3. Nature____the land for itself in the 60 years since the war ended.
4. The land is the last____of Korea's natural state before humans.
5. Many people were____at the thought of____digging up the DMZ...
6. ...to build gas stations and____malls...
7. ...so they mapped out a____to preserve it.
8. Fifty-one species of animals have already been____out.

a. endangered
b. bulldozers
c. refuge
d. strip
e. horrified
f. wiped
g. strategy
h. uninhabited
i. remnant
j. reclaimed

Answers on page 160.

DISCUSS

1. Do you agree that the DMZ should be preserved as a natural wildlife preserve? Which of these statements best describes the way you feel? Tell why you think so.
   a. It should be kept as a natural reserve for endangered species of animals and plants.
   b. Just a small part of it should be turned into a wildlife preserve.
   c. It should be used to build new apartments and businesses.
2. Would it bother you if the DMZ is invaded by construction companies bulldozing the land and cutting down the trees and chasing all the animals away?
   a. That would be a nightmare to me.
   b. Of course it would make me sad, but that's life.
   c. I have no problem with building apartments, stores, and gas stations in the DMZ.
3. Where do you think the Korean citizens stand on the issue of preserving the DMZ as a natural wildlife preserve? Tell why you think so.
   a. Most Koreans care about wildlife and will choose to preserve the DMZ.
   b. Most Koreans will want to develop the DMZ just like the rest of the country, with apartment buildings, shopping malls and gas stations.
4. What do you think about environmentalists from foreign countries getting involved in the fight to save the DMZ? Does it make you feel good, or do you think it is none of their business? Tell why you think so.
5. It has also been suggested that the DMZ be turned into an international peace park after reunification. What do you think of that idea? What would you do with all the animals living there?

DMZ Peace Park?

6. The only leaders on the Korean peninsula ever to express a concern for preserving the DMZ were two old leaders— Kim Young Sam and Kim Jong Il. So do older Koreans care more about the saving the environment than younger Koreans do?
7. Are you an environmentalist? If so, what do you do to protect the environment?
8. Some of the animals living in the DMZ are dangerous to humans. What should be done with them if the DMZ is opened up for travel? Tell why you think so.
   a. Put up high fences beside the roads and let them run free, the same as now.
   b. Capture them and put them in zoos. c. Move them to other countries.

Environment

UNIT 27 The KTX vs. Nature

When the KTX bullet train began operation in 2004 Korea became only the fifth nation in the world to offer travelers high speed rail service, the other countries being France, Germany, Spain, and Japan. When KTX service began it was hailed as the biggest national policy project since the founding of Korea. The total cost to build the KTX was about 18.5 trillion won (US$14 billion), by far the most expensive national project ever undertaken by the Korean government.

Few people complained about the money being spent because cutting travel time around the country was badly needed. Seventy percent of the population of Korea lives along the corridor between Seoul and Busan. Seventy-five percent of the nation's GDP is generated there.

"The KTX was...the most expensive national project ever undertaken by the Korean government."

One of the negative side effects of Korea's exponential growth over the past two decades has been a surge in road traffic accompanied by a huge drop in air quality. Congestion along the Seoul-Busan corridor had slowed to a crawl during busy periods. By getting some of the vehicles off the roads, building the KTX was another step toward improving Korea's environment.

Korean bullet train

Environment

Vocabulary

- **(be) hailed as**: to be praised as...
- **(be) undertaken**: (a job or task) being attempted
- **corridor**: a long, narrow passage
- **GDP**: gross domestic product, the value of all goods and services produced in a year
- **(be) generated**: is produced by factories and businesses
- **exponential growth**: extremely rapid growth
- **surge**: sudden increase
- **congestion**: very crowded condition
- **slowed...crawl**: moving very slowly

Besides making commuting between Seoul and cities in the south much faster, the KTX plays an important role in the movement of freight, which in turn helps the country economically.

By absorbing the lion's share of the passenger traffic between Seoul and the southern ports, the transport of freight shifted from road traffic to existing train lines. Since the KTX has gone into service the number of containers moved per year has jumped 900 percent from just 350,000 previously to 3 million today.

Traveling on the 300 km./hr. KTX is a dream come true for people who prefer to travel by train, but the comforts don't come cheap. The initial passenger fares were set at 25% higher than the first class fares on the older lines. A ticket between Seoul and Busan is now 57,300 won*, considerably higher than the fare on the older first-class Saemaeul line.

KTX driver's cab

A KTX terminal resembles an airport.

Conveniences provided on the KTX but never before available to passengers on older Korean trains include vending machines for drinks and snacks, and a video/audio system.

Train reservations can be made up to two months in advance on the Internet, and KTX train terminals rival international airports in terms of facilities and services.

*fare in 2013

KTX passenger compartment

3 million containers moved per year

Vocabulary

- **freight**: manufactured goods
- **the...share**: the majority of, most of
- **don't...cheap**: are expensive
- **rival**: are just as good as

Environment

Naewon Temple, located on Mt. Cheonseong

As with nearly most other public projects ever undertaken in Korea, construction of the KTX was also a source of controversy. In 2001 a battle flared up between the government and environmentalists over the construction of a 13.2-km.-long tunnel under Mt. Cheonseong in South Gyeongsang Province.

Environmentalists were worried that the tunnel would damage the underground water system and dry up swamps, destroying the habitat of 11 animal species on the endangered list, in particular, the long-tailed salamander, which ended up becoming the focus of the fight.

Although the Ministry of the Environment had already conducted an environmental evaluation in 1994, concluding that the tunnel would not have a detrimental effect on the mountain's ecosystem, conservationists weren't so sure.

Several environmental groups, along with the Buddhist nuns from the Naewon Temple, located on Mt. Cheonseong, sued the Ministry of the Environment on behalf of the salamander, and the court case became known as the "Salamander Trial." It was the first time in Korean history that an animal filed a suit against anyone in court.

During the trial, several thousand people testified on the salamander's behalf, but the court concluded that the salamander didn't have a good case, and construction of the tunnel was allowed to go forward. Angry over having lost the case, one of the Buddhist nuns went on a hunger strike, and tunnel construction was temporarily shut down. But the KTX won the battle, and the tunnel was completed. The KTX went into operation in March of 2004.

The first animal to sue a government agency

Environment

Vocabulary

- **swamp**: a wet area where only some water-loving plants and animals can live
- **habitat**: place where they live
- **focus**: main point of interest
- **environmental evaluation**: do a study of the impact on the environment
- **detrimental effect**: do some damage
- **ecosystem**: relationship between plants, animals, natural environment
- **weren't...sure**: didn't believe it
- **on behalf of**: instead of

WORD PRACTICE

Fill in the correct word.

1. 70% of Koreans live in the____between Seoul and Busan...
2. ...and 75% of the____is generated there.
3. Korea has experienced____growth in the past 2 decades.
4. ____along the route caused traffic to slow to a____on weekends.
5. The train plays an important role in the movement of____.
6. The train provides many comforts, but they don't come____.
7. KTX terminals____airports when it comes to services.
8. Many people thought that the tunnel would have a____effect...
9. ...on the mountain's____, but they turned out to be wrong.

a. exponential
b. crawl
c. congestion
d. GDP
e. rival
f. corridor
g. ecosystem
h. detrimental
i. cheap
j. freight

Answers on page 160.

DISCUSS

1. Do you remember hearing about the salamander trial? If so, which side were you on—the government's or the environmentalists'? Which of these statements best describes your feelings about the case?
   a. The environmentalists and Buddhist nuns were right. Protecting nature is more important than any railroad tunnel.
   b. The government was right. Protecting nature should not stand in the way of progress.

2. If the environmental evaluation of Cheonseong Mountain conducted by the Ministry of the Environment had concluded that building the tunnel WOULD have damaged the ecosystem of the mountain, what do you think should have been done? Tell why you think so.
   a. In that case, the tunnel should not have been built.
   b. That's too bad. The tunnel would still have to be built.

KTX tunnel

3. What do you think of the method taken by the Buddhist nun to stop the construction of the tunnel--a hunger strike? Do you think this is a good way to protest a governmental decision? Why or why not?
4. If the government decided to build a highway where your house was and told you to move, what would you do? Would you go on a hunger strike? Sue the government? Would you move?
5. Where should the line be drawn between what is best for nature and what is best for the convenience of society? Should there be any limit at all? Tell why you think so.
   a. There shouldn't be any limit on construction. Whatever is needed by the people is more important than the needs of nature.
   b. There should be a limit. If a new building project is going to destroy the natural habitat of an endangered species of animal, then that project should be cancelled.
6. What grade do you give the Korean government for their concern for the environment—A, B, C, D, or Fail? When new construction projects are made, how much consideration is given to how that project will affect the environment?
7. How much did the building of the KTX improve the environment in Korea? —a lot, a little, not at all. Tell why you think so.
8. Do you think the KTX was worth all the money that it cost to build and operate?

UNIT 28 Cars vs. Clean Air

Seoul: Then.... ....and Now

Just one generation ago it was the dream of almost every man in Korea, young or old, to have his own car. Wages were low, and owning a car was outside the reach of the average person. Almost all the vehicles on the roads were buses, taxis or government vehicles. The only people who owned cars were rich company executives or government officials so a car was more a sign of wealth than a necessity.

In 1979 there were fewer than 200,000 cars in all of Korea. There was so little road traffic that a person could jaywalk across any one of Seoul's downtown's streets without having to worry about getting run over.

All of that has changed of course. Today cars are more a necessity of life than a status symbol, and the roads are packed. There has also been a huge trade-off—convenience for an air-polluted environment.

"...a person could jaywalk...without having to worry about getting run over."

Back then Korean cities had blue skies and clean air to breathe, but on some days today there is a noticeable layer of brown smog hanging over them. Although much improvement in air quality has taken place since 2000, Korean skies are still not as blue as they were 2 decades or so ago.

Jaywalking in the1970s—very safe!

Vocabulary

- **(be) outside...of**: most people couldn't afford one
- **more...necessity**: didn't really need one, just wanted to have one to show off
- **to jaywalk**: cross the street where there is no crosswalk, just cross anywhere
- **(be) packed**: bumper to bumper, covered with cars
- **tradeoff**: give up one thing in order to get something else
- **smog**: a mixture of smoke and dirt that makes the air hard to see through (like fog)

Environment

It is hard to see a light at the end of the tunnel for cleaning up Korea's air pollution. That's because Koreans are not about to give up their cars or their car industry anytime soon.

Cars are too important to the Korean economy. The country is the 5th largest producer of automobiles in the world, and the auto industry is responsible for much of Korea's wealth. In other words, Korea's air is polluted not only by all the cars on the roads but also by the factories that make them.

Drive to work in this, or take the bus?

"Not many Koreans can bear the shame of not owning a car."

It's also still too soon after the days when most Koreans were too poor to buy a car. Now that they can afford them, how many Koreans would be willing to give up their cars and go back to taking the bus? Nobody.

Probably the most important reason why Koreans will not give up their cars is simply because a car is now a necessity of life. Although the kind of car a person drives still carries weight with neighbors and colleagues, the most important thing is just having one. Not many Koreans can bear the shame of not owning a car.

Of course, the Korean government has been trying to find ways to clean up the air. One of them is to limit the amount of sulfur dioxide that factories can give off. Japan, whose air is also polluted, has been working with Korea to work on a joint solution.

Pollution blown in by the wind from China is part of the problem, but according to the 2007 study, 74 to 90 percent of the dry deposits of acid on the ground is produced inside Korea.

The KLI 63-Bldg in 1988 against a deep blue sky. *(Yes, it really DID look like that!)*

Vocabulary

- **light...tunnel**: be able to see a solution coming soon
- **(be) about to**: are not going to (do something)
- **necessity of life**: something a person can't live without
- **still...weight**: it's important, it matters
- **bear...shame**: be embarrassed because...
- **joint solution**: a solution that both think of together

Korea used to have deep blue skies. No more.

There isn't anybody in Korea under the age of 40 who would say that the development of a car culture in Korea has been all good, because that wouldn't be true. Of course having your own car certainly beats waiting for a bus in the rain, but when everybody else has a car too, it creates a problem.

Sulfur dioxide emissions in South Korea are 10 times higher than in the north.

Time wasted due to traffic congestion aside, the people's health is increasingly at risk. The number of cars on Korea's roads has gone up from just 100,000 in 1969 to around 15 million today. Of course, Koreans love their cars, but those cars have had a devastating effect on the air that they breathe, especially in the big cities.

The amount of carbon dioxide being put into the air by all the cars is rising at a dangerous rate, and more and more people are being diagnosed with respiratory conditions. School absenteeism, heart attacks, and premature death are all on the rise. All are due to the dirty air.

Air pollution in Korea has reached a dangerous level. A study released by the National Institute of Environmental Research in 2007 reported that the emission of **sulfur dioxide** (SO_2) in Korea was 4 times higher than the level recorded on Japan's west coast and 10 times higher than the level in the north.

SO_2 is produced by burning oil and coal and is what causes acid rain The more pollution in the air, the more acid in the rain. Acid rain kills trees, kills fish, destroys buildings and makes people sick.

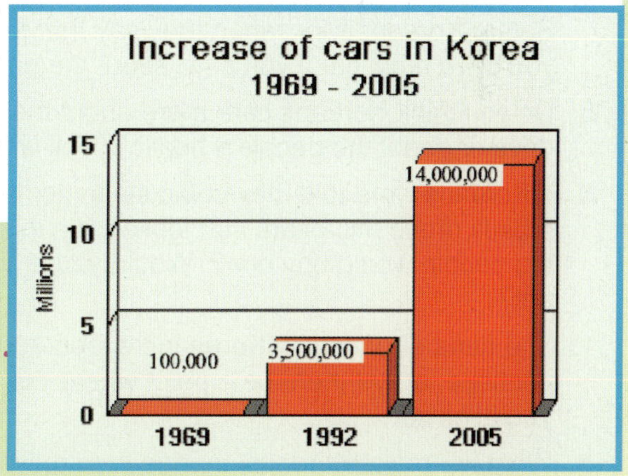

Vocabulary

- **beats**: is much better than
- **...aside**: in addition to...
- **(be) at risk**: is in danger of being harmed
- **devastating**: extremely damaging
- **(be) diagnosed (with)**: found to be infected with...
- **respiratory conditions**: breathing problems
- **premature death**: dying sooner than should be expected
- **acid rain**: sulfur dioxide is dissolved by the water droplets in clouds

WORD PRACTICE

Fill in the correct word.

1. In the 1980s owning a car was outside the____of most Koreans.
2. Cars used to be____symbols, but today they're a____of life.
3. In the 1970s____was very safe and you could do it anywhere.
4. Not many Koreans can bear the____of not owning a car.
5. There has been a huge____of clean air for convenience.
6. Japan and Korea are trying to find a____solution to the problem.
7. Having your own car____waiting for a bus in the rain.
8. More and more Koreans are being____with____conditions.

a. reach
b. trade-off
c. respiratory
d. status
e. joint
f. diagnosed
g. necessity
h. beats
i. jaywalking
j. shame

Answers on page 160.

DISCUSS

1. Can you remember when there were not so many cars on Korean roads? How has Korea changed since those days? Was the sky bluer than it is today?
2. Do you own a car? If so, how long have you owned it, and why did you buy it:? Do you think of your car as a status symbol or a necessity of life?
3. When Koreans buy new cars which of the following factors carries the most weight in their decision on which car to buy? Rank them in importance from 1 to 5. Explain your choices.
   - Functionality (how well the car meets their needs—carrying capacity, comfort, etc.)
   - Durability (how many years they can drive the car without having to buy a new one)
   - Economy (how energy efficient the car is, how little gas it will use)
   - Value (getting the most features for the least amount of money)
   - Luxury (the car's ability to impress other people)
4. Koreans say they are worried about global warming but they still like to drive big cars. So are Koreans lying when they say that they care about the environment? How can you drive a big car if you care about the environment?.
5. Do you think Koreans care more about the kind of car that they drive or about the people's health? Tell why you think so.

6. If Koreans were told they could clean up their air by 80% if everybody drove microcars that looked like this, what percentage of the people would buy one? Would you drive one? Why or why not?
7. The number of cars in Korea increased 400% between 1992 and 2005. Will this trend continue, or will there be a point where the number of cars stops increasing? Tell why you think so.
8. What will make Koreans change their driving habits? Tell why you think so.
   a. ...when family members start having breathing problems
   b. ...when polluted air makes them drive with the headlights on during the daytime
   c. ...when the price of gas goes to 15,000 won per liter

9. What should be done to solve the problem? Should the price of gasoline be raised 3 or 4 times to stop people from buying cars? Will Koreans make changes to their lifestyle to clean up their air, or will they refuse? Tell why you think so.

UNIT 29

Hi-Tech Korea

Future Songdo City in Incheon

Koreans have taken to high tech like ducks take to water. They're up to their ears in electronic gadgets, and they love it. They can't seem to get enough.

In any high tech competition, whether it be high-speed Internet access or the percentage of the population with cell phones,

> "...the only untapped market is the kindergarten to first-grade segment."

Korea ranks at or near the top. With a population of just 48.6 million, Korea had 40 million Internet subscribers and 45.6 million cellular phones in 2013. That's 93% coverage and one of the highest cell phone saturation rates in the world.

The vice president of Qualcomm Internet Services Korea, Park Mun Seo, was quoted in 2006 as saying, "I think the only untapped market is the kindergarten to first-grade segment."

Underscoring Korea's commitment to turning itself into the hi-tech capital of the world is New Songdo City, a ubiquitous city now being constructed near Seoul. The goal is to eventually link all computers in houses, hospitals, businesses, and government together to share data.

The preferred language spoken is to be English, but achieving that goal has been difficult. It's been hard to attract enough native speakers to work and study in that remote and inconvenient location so far from any major city.

Vocabulary

- **taken...water**: have adapted very well, feel very comfortable with it
- **be up...ears**: have so much of it
- **gadgets**: devices. communication tools
- **Internet subscribers**: people who have Internet accounts in their homes
- **cell...rates**: percentage of the population that has one
- **untapped market**: age group still not using cell phones
- **ubiquitous city**: All information is accessible and shared by all computers

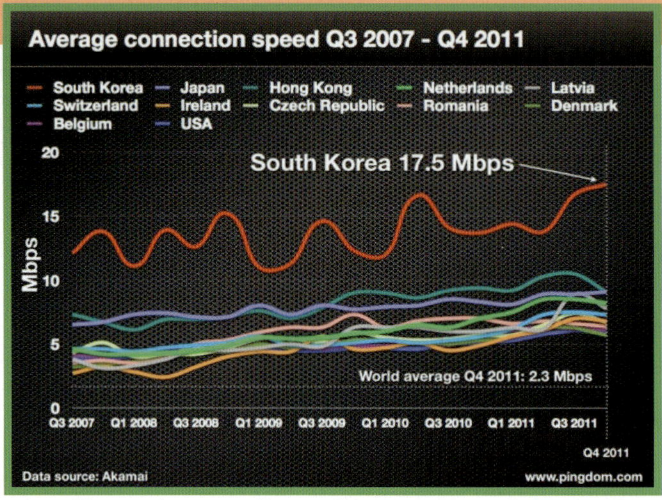

The world has entered an era of I.T., and Korea has become one of its leaders. Thanks to a 1998 government plan to set up a high speed communication network throughout the country, Korea is now the most wired countries in the world.

Between 1998 and 2000 a network of 22,000 km. of fiber optic cable linking 144 cities and towns was installed all across the country. In 2011 Korea continued to lead the world in Internet connection speed, with a wide gap between itself and 2nd place Japan (see chart above).

One example of how Korea is keeping up with the latest trends was the launching of IPTV (Internet TV) in 2006. IPTV requires very fast Internet connectivity in order to work properly, but that was not a problem for Korea, thanks to the network of fiber optic cable installed across the country 8 years earlier. Korea was in a position to adapt IPTV before most other countries in Asia even had the necessary infrastructure in place. Today Korea has connection speeds 10 times faster than the USA and twice as fast as Japan.

IPTV is the most important communication tool to come along since the Internet and television before that. IPTV is a combination of video on demand television, the telephone and the Internet all at the same time, and Korea was the first to have it.

In 2013 there were 6 million IPTV subscribers in Korea.

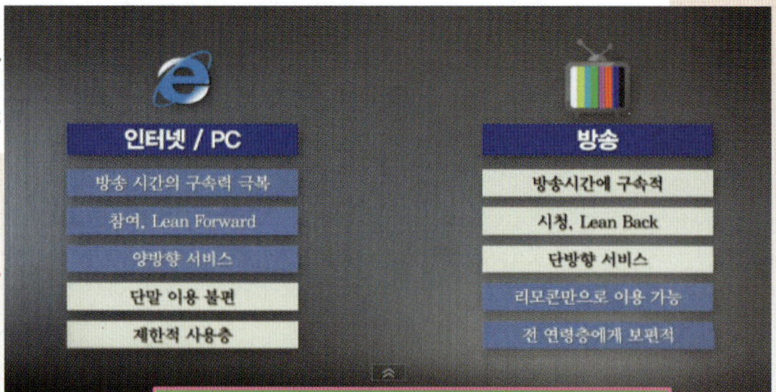

IPTV combines TV and the Internet controlled with a remote.

Vocabulary

- **era...IT**: the age of information technology
- **network**: many locations all linked together
- **fiber...cable**: lines capable of carrying digitized data over long distances very fast
- **keeping...trends**: adopting all the newest I.T. inventions
- **IPTV**: Internet Protocol Television (also called "Smart TV")
- **infrastructure**: the required equipment and fast internet connection network
- **video on demand (VoD)**: watch whenever you want to, not depending on any TV programming schedule
- **a remote**: a hand-held remote controller

A lot of the credit for Korea's high standing in the world of technology is owed to its high tech manufacturing sector which has developed from very humble beginnings in the late 1970s.

Four industry giants in particular—Samsung Electronics, LG Electronics, Korea Telecom and SK Telecom—have not only earned excellent names for themselves around the world as high-tech innovators but have enhanced Korea's productivity reputation in the world in the process.

In 2006 LG Electronics introduced the world's first TV-PC combo, allowing users to watch TV and surf the internet at the same time.

In 2012 Samsung outsold every other maker of digital TVs, LED-LCD TVs, and flat screen TVs in the US market, and it continued to be the most prestigious name in electronics across most of SE Asia.

Samsung introduced the first 3-D LED TV in 2010

Robot combatants will do the dangerous jobs.
Photo: Korea Times

Every aspect of Korean life has gone hi-tech, even the military.

There are unmanned aerial vehicles and submarines now patrolling the skies and seas for signs of infiltration by the North Korean military, and the army is developing reconnaissance "robot combatants" to replace live soldiers in dangerous places like the DMZ.

The robots will be used to patrol, remove land mines and even shoot at the enemy if and when that becomes necessary.

Vocabulary

- **sector**: portion of the country's total workforce
- **humble beginnings**: they began as very small companies
- **earned...themselves**: became well-known for their high quality products
- **innovators**: often introducing new and creative products
- **prestigious**: the brand that every consumer wants to have
- **infiltration**: invasion, coming in secretly
- **reconnaissance**: be the first to enter enemy territory and collect information
- **combatants**: fighters

WORD PRACTICE

Fill in the correct word.

1. Koreans are up to their____in hi-tech____.
2. Korea has one of the highest cell phone____rates in the world.
3. Five and six year olds may be the only____market in the country.
4. Korea has a hi-speed communication____throughout the country.
5. Koreans are determined to keep up with the latest hi-tech____.
6. LG and Samsung have earned____as high-tech____.
7. Samsung is the most____name in electronics throughout Asia.
8. The Korean army now has robot____to replace live soldiers.

a. saturation
b. trends
c. names
d. untapped
e. combatants
f. prestigious
g. ears
h. network
i. gadgets
j. innovators

Answers on page 160.

DISCUSS

1. Samsung advertises that their "Smart TV" has the power "to change the world". Do you agree with them? Tell why you think so.
   a. Yes, it will change the world because…
   b. I don't think any one product can change the entire world.
2. What explains why Koreans have adapted themselves to high tech so willingly, even though they are very conservative about most other things? Tell why you think so.
3. Is there a downside (negative side) to high tech? Has Korean society suffered in any way because of its rapid adaptation of high tech?
4. What social problems now exist that would not exist if the country were not so focused on high technology?
5. Is it possible for a traditional Confucist way of thinking to exist in a high tech modern world? If not, then what is going to happen to Korea's traditions and culture? Isn't it going to change?
6. If Korean society changes because of its acceptance of high tech into every aspect Korean life, will that be a good thing or a bad thing? Tell why you think so.
7. 93 percent of Koreans have cell phones, a much higher percentage than even the USA. Why does almost every Korean, young or old, have a cell phone while only 63% of Americans have one? Is there something about Korean life that makes having a cell phone an absolute necessity? If so, what?
8. How old were you when you got your first cell phone? Why did you get it?
9. What do you think about young elementary school children—6-9 years old—having cell phones?
10. How will the South Korean high tech military equipment affect the standoff with the North, which will not have the money to build the same hi-tech equipment?
    a. It will make it impossible for the North to invade the South, so the North will have to give up.
    b. It will just make the North angrier and more determined to invade the South.

Country	% of pop. with cell phones*
So. Korea	93
Australia	79
Japan	74
USA	63
Thailand	44
China	25
India	6

*2012 Statistics

UNIT 30 Internet Addiction

It's hard to argue that Korea's rapid rate of Internet connectivity can be anything but an asset to the country. It has already paid off as Korea's reputation as a high technology powerhouse is well established around the world.

By 2005 Korea was the first country to complete the conversion from dial-up to broadband, and in 2013 Korea had the world's highest per capita DSL Internet connection rate with more than 94% of Korean households having fast Internet access. 37 million out of Korea's 45 million people now use the Internet.

But there is also a dark side to cyberspace, and it is called Internet addiction—a mental disorder that affects more people in Korea than in any other country. It is the inability to know when to turn off the computer.

A survey taken in 2003 found that 41% of Korean middle and high school students showed some symptoms of Internet abuse. Becoming addicted to the Internet is probably the biggest danger facing Korean young people today. The popularity of hand-held devices like iPhones and tablet computers has made the problem even worse.

This PC room even lists it's computer specs

Vocabulary

- **connectivity**: being connected to the Internet
- **asset**: something helpful, to one's benefit
- **conversion...band**: connecting to the Internet by a cable line instead of by phone
- **highest...rate**: high number of people who are using it
- **Internet access**: can connect to the Internet from home
- **symptoms**: signs, indications of a problem
- **Internet abuse**: being harmed by the use of the Internet
- **specs**: *specifications* (details about the computers' power)

Hi-Tech

Young Koreans are drawn to the Internet for two main reasons—gaming and pornography. The first of these, gaming, is a phenomenon in Korea, and it attracts many males between the ages of 15 and 30. In 2013 one-third of the Korean population were gamers.

But too much gaming can be deadly. In 2002 a 25 year old died of heart failure after playing online games for 86 hours straight eating nothing but instant noodles for 3 days. Another young man died in 2005 doing the same thing.

Pornography, prostitution, and sex. The other big draw for Koreans involves online text and video chatting. More than 10 million Koreans participate in text chatting and about 1 million in video chatting. Most of the chatting is about sex. That has created a whole new set of problems for Korean society.

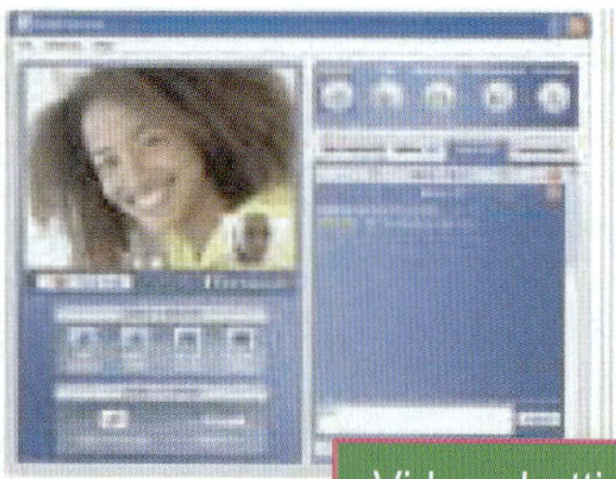

Video chatting lets you see what your friend looks like

Thanks to the Internet, teenagers can now look at pornographic pictures any time they want to. As a result, teenage prostitution is increasing, and married women who are unsatisfied with their husbands are having sex with strangers on the side.

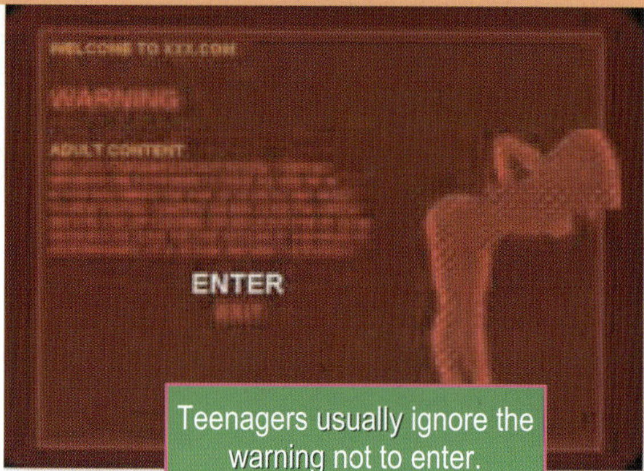

Teenagers usually ignore the warning not to enter.

Connection addiction. Handheld devices like tablet computers, iPhones, and Android devices have extended the reach of the Internet, so that there is never any need to be offline as long as wi-fi is available. One writer has described it as *"the need to be [cyber]-connected through a continual diet of texting, tweeting, instant messaging (SMS) and other interactive on-line activity."** If you check your email again 10 minutes after you just checked it, you're addicted.

Addicted: PC, laptop, tablet, iPhone, all at the same time

Vocabulary

- **gaming**: playing computer games with other people over the Internet
- **pornography**: pictures or videos showing people having sex
- **straight**: without stopping
- **draw:** thing that makes them want to go there
- **strangers**: men that they've never met before, unknown to them previously
- **on the side**: secretly, outside of their marriage
- **interactive...activity**: communicating with others through wireless devices like cell phones or computers

*source: atyourlibrary.com, Wanda Urbanski

A Korean "PC Bang" Cybercafe

Internet addiction affects certain types of people more than others. Shy people are much more susceptible than people who are active and outgoing. Teenagers who become addicted are almost always unpopular at school and have very few friends. They exhibit anti-social behavior and get more pleasure out of playing online games at home than hanging out with friends.

The online activities that hook most addicts are gaming, instant messaging, pornography, and chat rooms.

Internet addiction is such a big problem in Korea that the government has gotten involved. By 2006 two branches of the Center for Internet Addiction Prevention and Counseling (CIAPC) had already opened, and by 2010 three more were added.

In 2007 a startup company called Xtive came up with an interesting new way to treat gaming junkies. After the gamer has spent a certain period of time at the machine, a sound containing a subliminal message starts to play. The message tells him to stop playing. The player is not aware of the message, but his subconscious is. Xtive says it really works.

Connection Addiction

(c) WWW.OHMYGOODNESS.COM

Connection addiction in the USA.

Vocabulary

- **(be) susceptible**: easily able to be affected
- **anti-social behavior**: don't like people very much
- **hook (be hooked)**: become addicted to it
- **startup**: new company
- **subliminal message**: the message is hidden inside the music

WORD PRACTICE

Fill in the correct word.

1. Korea has a really high rate of Internet____.
2. 41% of Korean h.s. students showed____of Internet____.
3. The popularity of____devices makes it even worse.
4. One young man died after playing a game for 3 days____.
5. Bored housewives are having sex with strangers on the____.
6. Online gaming and pornography are both big____for Koreans.
7. Nobody ever has to be____as long as wi-fi is available.
8. Shy people are especially____to Internet addiction.
9. ____messages may help make addicts turn off the computer.

a. abuse
b. straight
c. subliminal
d. symptoms
e. susceptible
f. draws
g. connectivity
h. offline
i. side
j. hand-held

Answers on page 160.

DISCUSS

1. What do you think about this problem? Are you internet or connection addicted?
   a. I think it's terrible, and yes, I'm probably addicted.
   b. I'm addicted, but I think it's fine.
   c. Big problem, and I'm definitely not addicted. I use computers and handheld-devices as little as possible.

2. Which wireless devices do you own, and how often do you use them?
   a. PC or laptop.
   b. iPad or Android (Samsung) tablet and/or iPhone
3. In 2007 four 6th grade students (11 years old) had sex after looking at pornography websites in their classroom. Would any of the following measures help? If not, then what?
   a. Require teachers to stay in the classroom with students at all times.
   b. Block all pornography websites from Korea.
   c. Don't teach students about the Internet until they are in high school.
   d. Nothing. It's only natural for kids to experiment with new things like sex.
4. Is it possible that Korea has developed its world-famous IT industry too fast without thinking of the consequences of Internet addiction? Could it be said that Korea's rush to become the world's first wired country was a mistake? Tell why you think so.
5. Wireless broadband (WiBro) makes it possible for Koreans to connect to the Internet with their notebooks and hand-held devices everywhere they go, twenty-four hours a day. Will this lead to more Internet addiction in Korea than there already is, or will it make no difference? Tell why you think so.
6. Korea has the highest percentage of broadband Internet users in the world, and it also has the highest rate of Internet addiction. Do you agree that Korea is paying too high a price for having so much connectivity to the Internet? Tell why you think so.
7. What do you think of Xtive's subliminal message method of making gamers stop gaming? Is it a good idea? Do you think it can work? Why or why not?
8. In Thailand every first grade student (6 years old) is given a tablet computer when he or she starts school. Do you think that's a good idea? Would you like to see that happen in Korea too? Why or why not?
9. Is there any danger that students who spend too much time communicating online may not develop the necessary social skills needed to interact with people in face-to-face situations?

UNIT 31 eCommerce in Korea

There is no way that today's I.T. revolution is changing the way Koreans live any more than the sudden increase in online shopping, commonly known as eCommerce. The people who sell things on the Internet are called eMerchants, and people who buy things are called online shoppers.

More and more Koreans are flocking to the Internet as a place to purchase everything from computer software to imported goods they'd never be able to afford in a department store. They're even buying imported cars. The Korea Times reported that monthly sales of Bidbuy.com, an eCommerce site specializing in Japanese goods, doubled from 2005 to 2006. Sales of Wizwid, the largest overseas shopping site in Korea, grew by 35% during the same period.

One factor driving online sales was the strengthening of the Korean won compared to the US dollar and the Japanese yen, but even more important has been Koreans' love affair with the Internet. Since Korea is one of the most wired countries in the world, Koreans are comfortable with all aspects of the Internet, of which one of the most progressive and innovative is online shopping.

Koreans like the convenience of online shopping and the fact that prices are usually much lower than the prices charged for the same items by regular stores.

Koreans love to shop online.

Vocabulary

- **be flocking to**: large number of people going there
- **goods**: products for sale, items
- **to specialize in**: concentrate on that type of products
- **strengthening...won**: Makes imported goods cost less in Korea
- **(be) wired**: be connected to the Internet in their homes
- **progressive**: advanced, very developed
- **innovative**: creative, always changing, improving

Interior of Mercedes S class: popular with high-end buyers

So much money can be saved by shopping online that it's almost foolish to shop anywhere else. A Sony digital camera that retails for 285,000 won in Korean stores might be available on Bidbuy for 203,000 won or less, a 30% savings.

An imported Mercedes Benz S Class car that retails for 270 million won at car dealers might be gotten for just 130 million won online. Who would be foolish enough to pay 270 million won to a dealer for the same car they can get online for less than half the price?

What sets Korean online shoppers apart from other online shoppers in the world is that Koreans are more interested in imported goods than things produced in their own country. That's because many products made in foreign countries are either hard to get or not available in Korean stores. This is the dream of high-end shoppers for whom money is no object.

Online shopping is more popular than discount stores.

Vocabulary

- **retails**: price charged by stores is the "retail price"
- **dealers**: businesses where cars are sold are called "car dealers"
- **sets...apart**: makes them different from other people
- **(be) hard to get**: hard to find, most regular stores don't sell it
- **high...shoppers**: rich people who want the best quality
- **money...object**: they have so much money that they can buy anything they want anytime they want

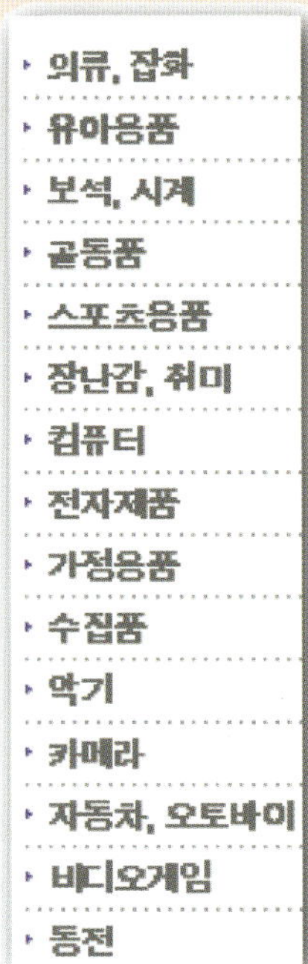

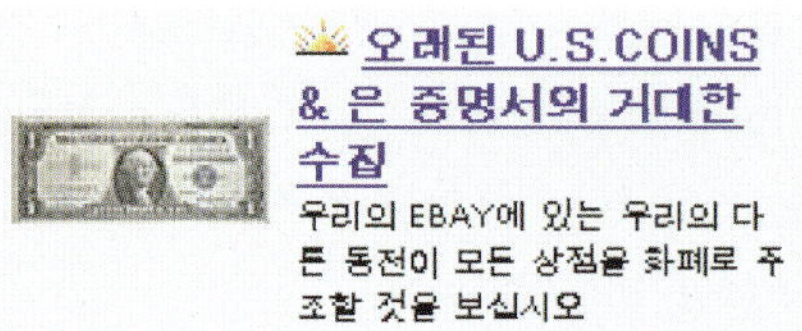

Koreans can buy anything online, even old American money.

Discount store

Online shopping is not totally a win-win situation for online shoppers, but the advantages outweigh the disadvantages. Reasons to shop online are:

1. The convenience of shopping from home
2. Much lower prices
3. A bigger selection of goods than any store could offer
4. No high pressure salesmen making you rush to a decision
5. Ability to compare all similar items

The disadvantages include:

1. Loss of the enjoyment of walking around a store
2. Having to give out personal information, such as name, address, and credit card number
3. Can't try on clothes or touch a product
4. Too many items to choose from

One possible side effect of online shopping in Korea is hastening the death of the Korean flee market, the shijang. The shijang was in trouble even before the Internet came along, attacked by discount stores that won the hearts of Koreans in the 1990s.

Lured by the convenience of one-stop shopping, indoor parking, and unbeatable prices, Koreans flocked to discount stores. One after another, shijangs were dismantled to make way for discount stores and their huge parking lots.

Online shopping is even more of a danger. The more Koreans spend shopping online, the less often they go out to shop. The less often they go out to shop the less likely they are to visit a shijang...or even a discount store.

Korean shijang.

Vocabulary

- **win...situation**: everything about it perfect, no way to lose
- **outweigh**: outnumber, (more advantages than disadvantages)
- **high...salesmen**: salespeople who try to make you buy something
- **to hasten**: make it happen sooner
- **win...Koreans**: they (Koreans) fell in love with them
- **Lured**: tempted, made them want to do it
- **dismantled**: taken down, removed

WORD PRACTICE

Fill in the correct word.

1. More and more Koreans have been____to the Internet to shop.
2. Ecommerce works well in Korea because it is so____.
3. Online shopping is one of the most____aspects of the Internet.
4. A product may be available online for 25% less than its____price.
5. Even car____are losing money because of online shopping.
6. Many imported products are____to get in Korean stores.
7. The____of online shopping____the disadvantages.
8. Many shijangs were____to make way for discount stores.
9. He's so rich that money is no____for him when he goes shopping.

a. hard
b. innovative
c. dismantled
d. advantages
e. object
f. wired
g. outweigh
h. retail
i. dealers
j. flocking

Answers on page 160.

DISCUSS

1. How do you explain Koreans' eagerness to flock to online shopping faster than people in most other Asian countries? What is unique about Korean society that makes eCommerce so popular here?
2. Have you ever bought anything online? If so, which of the following benefits of online shopping influenced you the most to shop online?
   - Convenience of shopping from home—Lower prices than in retail stores
   - The product I wanted couldn't be found in Korean stores (hard to get)
   - Bigger selection of products online than in regular stores
   - Can take my time (go slower) in deciding which item to buy, whereas in a store I have to decide quickly
   - Another reason (explain)
3. Why do many Koreans love imported goods so much? Why are they willing to pay more for an item that is made in a foreign country rather than buy a similar item that was made in Korea? Tell why you think so.
4. Will online shopping cause retail prices in Korean stores to fall or will it have no effect? Why would anybody pay 285,000 won to a department store for a camera that they can get online for just 203,000 won? Tell why you think so.
5. How do you feel about giving your personal information, such as name, address, telephone number, and credit card number over the Internet when you shop online? Are you worried about having your information stolen by hackers? Why or why not?
6. What effect, if any, will the discount stores and online shopping have on the traditional Korean markets (shijangs)? Will these markets eventually disappear? If so, how many years will it take for that to happen?
7. The article lists "too many items to choose from" as one of the disadvantages of online shopping. Do you agree that this is a problem, making it harder to decide which one to buy, or do you enjoy having dozens of products to choose from?
8. What is the future of online shopping in Korea? Will it continue to grow more and more popular, or will there come a time when Koreans decide they want to go back to the traditional ways of shopping? Tell why you think so.
9. Can you think of any items that you would NOT want to buy online? Tell why.

UNIT 32 Cyber-bullying

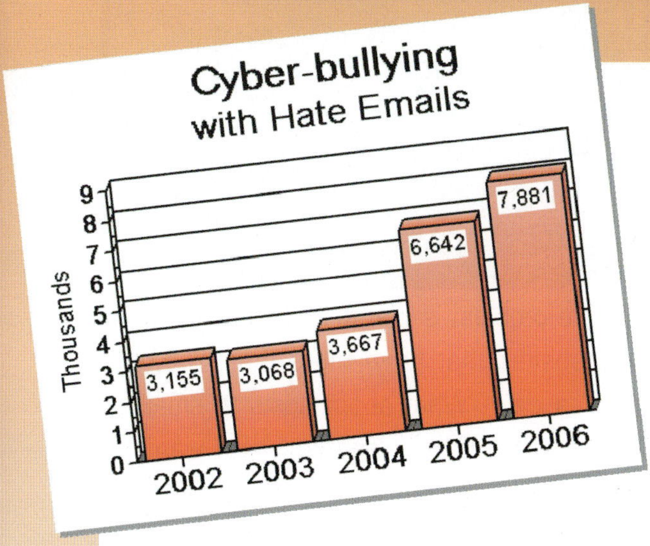

Most people would agree that email is one of the most important innovations in written communication in human history. Email makes it possible for people on opposite ends of the world to exchange thoughts and ideas almost as quickly as if they were in the same room.

Unfortunately, as with every other good invention, there will always be some people who will choose to abuse it, and email is no exception. In Korea the abusers are called "keyboard warriors", and their crime is cyber-bullying, the posting of malicious comments about people they don't like on Internet blogs. Since it started a few years ago, cyberbullying has become an epidemic in Korea. Why do blogs bring out the worst in people?

The effects of cyber-bullying can be tragic, as was learned in 2006 when a 26-year-old Korean pop singer killed herself after having been repeatedly insulted by keyboard warriors.

The anonymity of the Internet has made it possible for anyone to malign anybody else without having to worry about being caught. The number of hate emails posted on Korean blogs is rising very quickly.

Vocabulary

- **innovation**: improvement, modern invention
- **to abuse**: use it in a bad way, for the wrong reason
- **malicious**: hateful, harmful to others' feelings
- **blogs**: privately-operated websites where people can express their opinions
- **epidemic**: spreading, growing, increasing
- **bring...people**: make people do things they wouldn't ordinarily do
- **anonymity**: ability to remain secret, without having to give one's name
- **to malign**: say bad things about, to insult

Obviously, something has to be done about this problem. It cannot be allowed to go on unabated. Everybody except the keyboard warriors would agree. But the question is, what, if anything, can be done about it? Given the lack of control over the Internet and blogs in particular, is it even possible to stop cyber-bullying? Some people think it is.

Hoping to slow down the rising trend in cyber-bullying, Korea's Ministry of Information and Communication introduced an identification system in 2007 that required bloggers to identify themselves before being allowed to post any comments. Before that, In December of 2006 Korea's National Assembly passed a law making it mandatory for people to give their names and email addresses before they can post any comments on major blogs.

Blogs bring out the worst in people.

The problem is that that law applied only to websites that have more than 200,000 "hits" a day. What about posts to smaller, less popular blogs? The keyboard warriors can still have a field day on those websites slandering anybody they like without giving their names.

Another problem is that the rules of identifying website visitors differ from one blog to the next. Some blogs don't require users to give their real names.

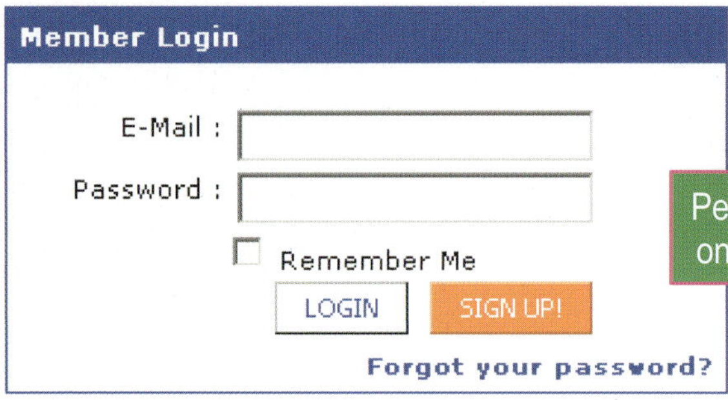

People who post messages on blogs have to login first.

Vocabulary

- **to go...abated**: continue without doing anything about it
- **(be) mandatory**: something that must be done, there is no other choice
- **to have...day**: enjoy themselves, have a good time doing it
- **to slander**: say terrible things about other people
- **real names**: their legal name, not a nickname
- **to login**: type your username or email address and password

Most Koreans who were surveyed about the new identification system said they thought it would be successful in reducing the amount of cyber-bullying going on, but at least 20% of them were skeptical. Some people predicted that the new system would just encourage people to use other people's names and email addresses, causing an increase in another Internet problem— identity theft.

Another problem is that not every keyboard warrior is afraid to give his or her name. Some people have no problem with letting others know who they are. How is it possible to stop people like that from cyber-bullying? The answer is, it may be impossible.

Most of the scandals that have resulted from cyber-bullying have originated from websites where bloggers give their real names. Even worse, some people don't even think that cyber-bullying is a problem. They believe that protecting the freedom of expression, guaranteed in the Korean constitution, is more important than stopping people from saying bad things about one another.

It could just be that cyber-bullying in Korea is here to stay.

Keyboard warriors like to remain anonymous.

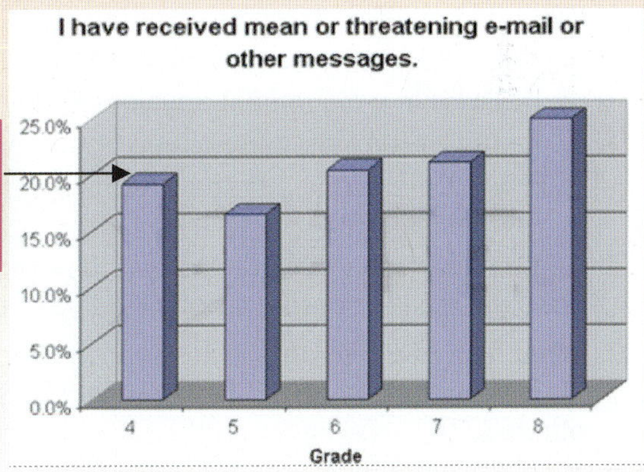

Cyber-bullying in the USA. Even 4th grade students (9-years-old) are being cyber-bullied.

Hi-Tech

Vocabulary

- **(be) surveyed**: answer questions in a survey (a poll)
- **to encourage**: make them more likely to do it
- **identity theft**: use another person's name and other personal information
- **have...with**: don't mind it, don't object, it's okay
- **originated**: began, started
- **freedom...expression**: a person's right to speak his or her opinion

WORD PRACTICE

Fill in the correct word.

1. Email is the most important____in written human communication.
2. Cyberbulling is the posting of____comments about other people.
3. It is____for people to give their real email addrsses before posting.
4. They're having a____day____people they don't like.
5. Some____don't require using your real name.
6. This can't be allowed to go on____,
7. The____of the Internet is what made this all possible.
8. Another huge Internet problem is that of____theft.
9. Some people have no____letting others know their real names.

a. mandatory
b. anonymity
c. slandering
d. identity
e. blogs
f. innovation
g. problem
h. malicious
i. unabated
j. field

Answers on page 160.

DISCUSS

1. How serious is the problem of cyber-bullying in Korea? Tell why you think so.
   a. It's a very serious problem that something must be done about.
   b. This is a free country. People should be allowed to say what they want about anybody they want.
2. Have you ever posted a comment on an Internet blog? What kind of a comment was it? Have you ever posted an insulting comment about anybody? If so, why did you do it?
3. Do you agree with the statement that Internet blogs bring out the worst in people? What makes some people say terrible things about people that they would not say if meeting the person face to face?
4. Do you think it is possible to stop cyber-bullying? Is it possible to stop it by passing laws against it? Why or why not?
5. What do you think about the new law requiring people to identify themselves before posting comments on a blog? Tell why you think so.
   a. It will have a big impact on cyber-bullying, reduce it quite a lot.
   b. It may help a little, but not very much.
   c. It won't make any difference at all because people can just sign in with other people's names instead of their own.
6. Some people don't mind attaching their real names to insulting comments about other people. Can keyboard warriors like this ever be stopped? Why or why not?
7. What type of a person is a keyboard warrior? Are they evil people? Are they lonely people? Why do they do it? Do they get pleasure out of hurting others?
8. Do you think most keyboard warriors are probably also Internet addicts—people who spend too much time online? Do you think there's any connection? Why or why not?
9. The parents of the pop star who killed herself want to sue the people who wrote the insulting comments. Do you think they will be successful? Why or why not?
10. Even after her death, the pop star was cyber-bullied by people who said they were glad she was dead. What do you think about that? What kind of person would write terrible things about a person even after they are dead? Are they mentally ill? Jealous? Insecure?

UNIT 33

Internet Gaming

Korea has become a land of opportunity and a proving ground for professional Internet gamers from all over the world. There are thousands of 24-hour Internet game rooms spread all across the country with several high-stakes competitions taking place at any one time. For the millions of gamers across the globe, Korea is a dream come true.

The reason why Korea has taken the lead in online gaming can be explained with just one word: broadband. Korea is the most wired nation in the world, with 70% of Korean homes having fast connections to the Internet, something that Internet gaming requires. It has made Korean gaming software companies global leaders in the industry and has drawn video game companies from other countries to Korea to try out their games on Korea's hoards of avid gamers.

Korea is now the center of MMORPGs (massively multi-player online role-playing games) where literally hundreds of thousands of players, represented by avatars, participate in adventure or historical fantasy games.

Nowadays young Korean gamers spend hours at cybercafes, known as PC Bangs, playing role-playing games like League of Legends and Diablo III. The World Cyber Games, which is the world's most prestigious worldwide gaming competition, held annually in different cities around the world, originated in Korea.

Diablo III: amazing landscapes

Hi-Tech

Vocabulary

- **high...competition**: games with very large prizes of money
- **dream...true**: a paradise, nothing better
- **taken...lead**: has become No. 1 in the world, the leader
- **broadband**: fast connection to the Internet (ADSL or cable)
- **hoards...gamers**: millions of young people who love online gaming
- **avatars**: animated characters that represent the gamers in the games
- **prestigious**: most important competition, winner becomes famous in the gaming world

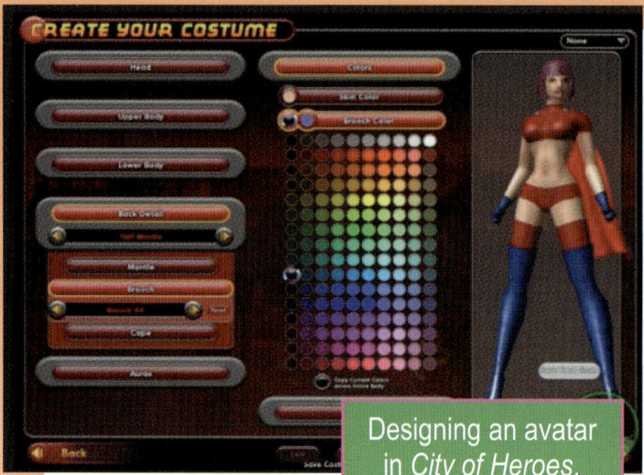

Designing an avatar in *City of Heroes*.

Today's Internet games are light years ahead of arcade games like Donkey Kong that came out in the 1990s. The new ones are a maze of fantasy worlds populated by real people representing themselves with realistic animated characters called avatars. Not only can players choose their own characters, but they can customize them by choosing the face, hair color, skin color, and hair style. It is their chance to have a body and appearance that a person can only dream about.

One huge difference between the gamers and their avatars is that their onscreen personalities have strength and powers that real human beings don't have. For gamers it is an exciting experience, and it helps explain why so many of them get hooked. They begin to identify with their avatars.

Since Korea's gaming rooms never close there is never a need to stop and go home. While unlimited gaming has its benefits, it can also be dangerous. Some gamers get so wrapped up in their alter egos and their fantasy worlds that they forget about their real worlds of school, jobs, and family. A few people have actually died from gaming overdose.

"A few people have actually died from gaming overdose."

The 1990s' Donkey Kong

Vocabulary

- **light years ahead**: extremely advanced
- **avatar**: a person's online image or character
- **onscreen personalities**: the characters that represent them in the games
- **get hooked**: become addicted to it, can't stop playing
- **to identify with**: start to think that they are that avatar
- **get...up**: they start to believe the fantasy world is their real world
- **alter egos**: online personalities, online "selves"
- **gaming overdose**: becoming physically weak or dying due to excessive playing

Besides being elaborate, most of the fantasy worlds inside the games are also enormous. The fantasy game, Lineage, has 50 different worlds, each of them so huge that it takes six hours just to walk from one end to the other.

Considering the exciting scenarios inside the fantasy games it's easy to see why Internet gaming has such enormous appeal for so many people. In a sense, the games are like action movies with the viewer actually participating in the action. It's just one step from actually stepping into the virtual reality world inside the screen .

While most online games like Lineage feature fantasy online role playing, others are just fighting competitions or center around sports, such as Soccer Fury, a game from NCSoft.

Internet gamers at play

Blade and Soul

Addiction. Unfortunately, there have been some problems. Internet addiction in Korea is an extremely serious problem, and gaming has caused Korea's high school dropout rate to soar.

Gambling. High stakes gambling, which is illegal in Korea, has also been linked to gaming. "The Sea Story" was shut down in 2006 because the video machines had been rigged to accept bets above the legal limit.

Lineage II: a world so large that it takes 6 hours to walk from one end to the other

Vocabulary

- **scenarios**: possible worlds, possible situations
- **virtual reality**: an illusionary world in which the viewer is inside the action
- **role playing**: pretending to be somebody else
- **to soar**: to increase to a high level very rapidly
- **high stakes**: betting large sums of money
- **rigged**: to manipulate fraudulently

WORD PRACTICE

Fill in the correct word.

1. Many high____gaming competitions take place in Korea
2. The World Cyber Games____in Korea in 2001.
3. Korea has taken the____in onling gaming around the world.
4. For gamers worldwide Korea is a____come true.
5. Today's games are____years ahead of the 90s' arcade games.
6. Players are represented in the games by their____.
7. Many players get all____up in their alter (online) personalities.
8. The world inside the games is one of____reality.
9. The exciting____inside the games have enormous____.

a. stakes
b. virtual
c. light
d. scenarios
e. wrapped
f. originated
g. avatars
h. appeal
i. dream
j. lead

Answers on page 160.

DISCUSS

1. How interested are you in Internet gaming? Do you have an avatar? Which one of these statements best describes how you feel about Internet gaming?
   a. I love gaming, I'm an expert gamer, and I have an avatar.
   b. I've watched others play, but I don't have time to play myself.
   c. I think online gaming is a waste of time, and the people who play are stupid.

WORLD Warcraft

2. What do you think about Korea being the gaming capital of the world? Are you impressed?
   a. I think it's great. It's a great honor for the country.
   b. Not good, It's childish, causes social problems.
3. Why have Koreans taken to online gaming faster than people in other countries? Why do they love online gaming so much?
4. The high school dropout rate has soared because of Internet gaming. Should gaming be banned in Korea? If not, what can be done to make students stop playing games long enough to study?
5. What do you think of the sexy imagery that is shown in some of the games? Is it contributing to the increased sex behavior of today's teenagers? Should the games be censored for violence and sexual content?

Blade and Soul: "2 sexy 4 kids?"

6. What is it about role-playing games that people find so fascinating? Why are they drawn to these games? Is it because they can be the type of character they cannot be in real life? Is this role type of playing the same as acting?
7. What type of people become addicted to Internet gaming? Are they lazy or very intelligent, creative people? Why do some people become addicts while others do not? What is the future of online gaming in Korea? Will Koreans eventually get bored with it and stop playing?
8. What is the best way to deal with family members who can't stop online gaming? Take away their computer?

UNIT 34 Digital Advertising

Telemarketing is either the best thing or the worst thing ever to come along in advertising since advertising was invented. It all depends on which end of the line you're on.

Businesses love it because they can reach an unlimited number of customers just by hooking up a live operator or a digitally recorded message to a computer that dials up phone numbers. Most recipients of telemarketing calls hate telemarketing because they see it as an invasion of their privacy. Another reason is that the calls usually come at very inconvenient times.

Most people hang up as soon as they realize they're talking with a computer, but only a very small percentage of people need to buy the service or product being sold for the calls to pay off. Korean telemarketers made 1.4 trillion won (US$15 billion) in Korea in 2007.

"Mobile phone are now the primary target of telemarketers."

landline phone

Telemarketing occurs the world over, but it has really exploded in Korea since the year 2000. Nobody is safe from these annoying calls anymore. It used to be that only landline phones were called, but since mobile phones now outnumber landlines in Korea, mobile phones are now the primary target of telemarketers.

Hi-Tech

Vocabulary

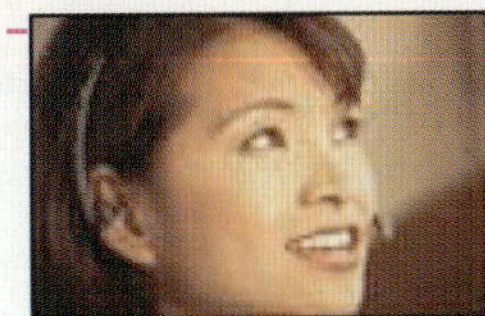
Live operator

- **telemarketing**: telephone advertisements
- **live** [rhymes with "five"] **operator**: a real human being
- **digitally...message**: a message which is on a computer
- **recipients**: the people who receive the calls
- **invasion...privacy**: receiving calls from people they don't even know
- **inconvenient times**: a time when you are busy or don't want to talk to anybody
- **pay off**: be successful (find someone to buy your product)
- **landline phones**: telephones in houses or offices

The other face of junk advertising comes in the form of unsolicited emails, otherwise known as *spam*. In 2011 the world's top 5 producers of spam were Iran, Nigeria, Kenya, Israel, and Canada, in that order, but Korea is also home to Internet hackers who steal personal information like email addresses or credit card numbers and then sell them for profit.

"Twenty percent of Koreans fell for scams..."

In 2004 fifteen Korean mobile phone workers earned 350 million won selling the personal information of 6 million people to spammers.

For the average email user, spam can be either just a nuisance or very dangerous. Hackers steal personal information through spam messages that look like they are from banks or credit card companies through a scheme called phishing.

In a spam message that looks like it's from a real bank, they tell the recipient that somebody has tried to use his or her account and that they need to type in their personal information again. If the user does that, the hackers steal that information. Twenty percent of Koreans fell for phishing scams in 2004.

In 2007 a 21-year-old computer science student at Daegu's Kyungbuk University who was nicknamed "spam queen" by Chosun Ilbo because of his "Kim Ha Na" emails was arrested for stealing the personal information of 12,000 Koreans and then selling it.

"MOM SAYS I CAN ONLY USE THE COMPUTER THREE HOURS A DAY. IT TAKES LONGER THAN THAT JUST TO DELETE MY SPAM!"

Hi-Tech

Vocabulary

- **unsolicited emails**: emails sent to people who didn't ask for them
- **hackers**: a person who illegally gains access to information on other computers
- **spammers**: people who send out the same email to huge number of people
- **nuisance**: something that is annoying
- **phishing** [sounds like "fishing"]: stealing personal data through emails that are disguised to look like they are from real banks or businesses.
- **to fall for**: believe something that is just a trick
- **scam**: a plan to steal money by tricking people

Telemarketing is mostly just a nuisance, but spam can be dangerous if somebody is gullible enough to fall for email scams that look like these.

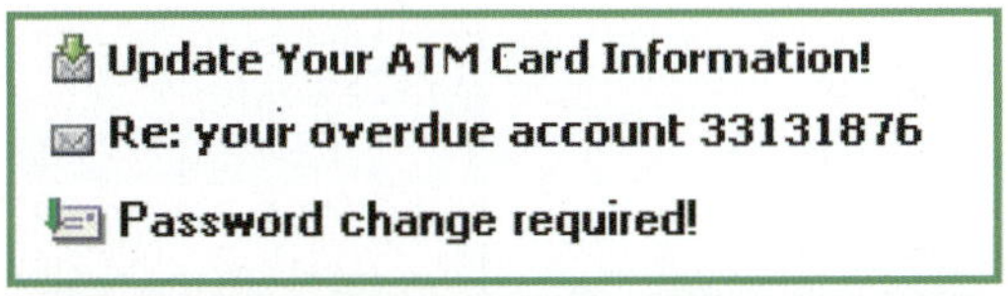

Do NOT open; just delete immediately!

There isn't a lot a person can do to stop the telemarketing calls, but it is possible to cut down on the amount of spam you get. The first rule is to avoid giving out your primary email address whenever possible. If you participate in chat rooms, set up a separate email account with Yahoo, Hotmail, or Daum.net especially for that purpose, and don't use your real name!

Read the privacy policy when you give your email address to a website. Check to see if it allows the company to sell your email address. When you join an e-mailing list, look for a promise that your email address won't be given to anyone else.

Anytime you give out your email address for any purpose, always read the webpage carefully before hitting the Submit button. Sometimes you have to uncheck a box to opt out of receiving advertisements.

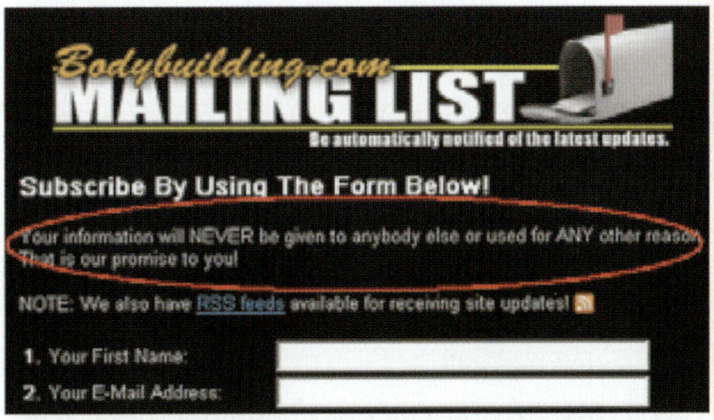

Use a different email address when subscribing.

Use a spam filter in your email program to automatically delete all emails that come in with certain words in their titles such as "money", "account" or "password". You will never be able to stop spam completely, but you can reduce it if you try.

Free web-based email accounts

Vocabulary

- **gullible**: foolish enough to believe that something is real when it's really a scam
- **cut...on**: to reduce
- **to give out**: to reveal, to let other people know about it
- **primary...address**: the email address where you receive your important emails
- **privacy policy**: every website that asks for email addresses should have one of these
- **Submit button**: the last button that you click to upload (send) your information
- **to uncheck**: the box will already be checked, you need to remove the check mark
- **to opt out of**: to let them know you don't want to receive email advertisements

WORD PRACTICE

Fill in the correct word.

1. Businesses can____up an operator or message to a computer.
2. Telemarketers can now call both____and mobile phones.
3. The calls have either a____operator or a digitally-____message.
4. Junk ads come in the form of____emails.
5. 20% of Koreans fall for____scams every year.
6. ____people can easily fall for email scams.
7. You should never give our your____email address.
8. Always read the____policy before giving out your email address.
9. You should always____out of receiving newsletters.

a. live
b. gullible
c. opt
d. phishing
e. primary
f. privacy
g. landline
h. unsolicited
i. recorded
j. hook

Answers on page 160.

DISCUSS

1. How do you feel about telemarketing calls?
   a. I hate them.
   b. They don't bother me.
   c. I like getting telemarketing calls.
2. How often do you receive telemarketing calls? Are the callers usually live operators or computers? If they are recorded messages, do you listen to them or hang up? If they are live operators what do you say?
3. Did you ever buy anything from a telemarketer? If so, tell about the experience.
4. Should laws be passed to limit or even stop telemarketing? Tell why you think so.
5. How do you feel about spam? Does it make you angry? How many spam messages do you receive per day, and what percentage of them do you read?
6. Have you ever bought anything because of a spam message? If so, tell about the experience.
7. In 2005 20% of all Korean Internet users (1 in 5) fell for (believed) a spam scam message and gave out their personal information to hackers. Were you one of those 20%?
8. Have you ever fallen for (believed) a spam message and given out your personal information by mistake? What do you think when you receive a message telling you to verify your personal information? What do you do with it?
9. Do you ever join memberships and mailing lists on the Internet? If so, do you read everything on the webpage before giving your name and email address or do you just fill in the form quickly and click "Submit"?
10. Do you participate in chat rooms? If so, do you use your own name or another name? Do you use your regular email address or another one? If so, why?
11. What kind of a person is an Internet scam artist—intelligent, greedy, a really bad person? Is there any difference between an Internet hacker and a bank robber? Tell why you think so.
12. How should hackers and scam artists be punished if they are caught? A fine? Jail time? How long?

UNIT 35

Korean Image Abroad

A tribute to the deaths of 32 Americans killed by a Korean-American in 2007.

Koreans care too much about what people in other countries think of them. Nothing illustrated that better than the reaction of Korean people after a mass murderer who happened to have been born in Korea massacred 32 people on a college campus in the USA in April of 2007.

Koreans, as everybody else, were understandably shocked and embarrassed, but Americans thought that they had overreacted. The Korean ambassador to the U.S. announced that he would fast for 32 days, one day for each of the shooting victims, and Koreans considered sending money to the families of the victims to compensate for their loss.

While these are nice gestures, they seemed bizarre to Americans who made no connection in their minds between the killer and Korea. The fact that the killer had been born in Korea was irrelevant, and Korea was not responsible.

The young man grew up in the United States and attended American schools from when he was 8, spoke fluent English, so they saw him as an American, not a Korean. He was just a troubled young man who had snapped. After the first day, US news reports didn't even mention that the killer was born in Korea. His ethnic background was not important to them.

No mention of the killer's ethnic background on US TV.

Vocabulary

- **mass murderer**: a person who kills many people
- **massacred**: murdered many people in a bad way
- **overreacted**: showed too much grief
- **compensate**: repay
- **bizarre**: extremely strange, hard to understand
- **(be) irrelevant**: not important to the situation
- **to snap**: suddenly behave in a very strange way

Political

Korean merchants living around the scene of the crime boarded up their stores, thinking they would be the targets of racial attacks. Korean students enrolled at the university were in fear of their

lives and moved around in groups for protection. Korean parents planning to send their children to study in the US cancelled their plans. All of these actions proved to be unnecessary. There was no backlash, and the expected attacks never happened.

The Korean Times printed an editorial accusing Koreans of projecting their own way of thinking onto Americans. If the situation were reversed, it said, and an American killed 32 Koreans, Koreans would probably blame all Americans. The fact that Americans didn't do that showed the big difference between Koreans and Americans.

The incident also showed how paranoid Koreans are about what foreigners think of them. They worry so much about how their country is being judged.

> "The incident showed how paranoid Koreans are about what foreigners think of them."

That might be because it wasn't until recently that Koreans could afford to think about such things. Until the mid-1980s Korea's primary focus was on the military situation with the North. Korea was just breaking out of poverty, and foreign visitors were rare.

That all changed with the 1986 Asian Games and the 1988 Summer Olympics in Seoul. With those two historic events, Korea's doors were swung wide open, and Korean tourism was born.

'88 Olympics

Boarded up for a backlash that never happened

Vocabulary

- **to board up**: cover windows and doors with wood
- **in...lives**: think they might be killed
- **backlash**: revenge, be punished for what the killer did
- **editorial**: newspaper's opinion
- **projecting...Americans**: assuming that Americans think the same way they do
- **paranoid**: be overly worried, to worry more than is necessary
- **primary focus**: main interest, the things they were concerned about the most
- **Korea's...open**: foreign tourists coming in large numbers for the first time

Street vendors were shut down in ′88.

People who are old enough to remember what the country's mood was like during the lead-up to the 1988 Olympics will remember how worried Koreans were about how their country was going to be depicted in the foreign media. News organizations from all over the world would be in the country with hundreds of reporters

> "Military bases were disguised as companies and the soldiers guarding them wore civilian clothes."

and TV cameras. And it was going to be Korea's first performance on the world stage since the Korean War, an event they desperately wanted to put behind them.

Koreans wanted to control where reporters could go and what their cameras could show, but they also knew that the foreign media wasn't used to having its hands tied. News organizations in western countries are used to being free to report anything they see, so if there were some things the Korean government didn't want to be exposed they'd have to hide them.

That's just what they did. During the Olympics, soldiers patrolling the streets wore jeans and T-shirts instead of military uniforms. Military bases were disguised as companies, and the soldiers guarding them wore civilian clothes. Koreans were afraid that the presence of soldiers and military bases would scare foreigners away.

Restaurants selling dog meat were closed in areas where foreigners were likely to visit, and street vendors (pojang-macha) were banned because foreigners might think they were unsanitary. Much has changed in the many years since 1988, but one thing that hasn't changed is how much Koreans worry about what foreigners think of them.

Most westerners are not used to seeing soldiers on patrol in public places.

Vocabulary

- **mood**: feeling, atmosphere
- **lead-up**: preparation period
- **(be) depicted**: be shown, described, characterized
- **put...them**: have it forgotten about, made a part of history
- **having...tied**: being restricted
- **(be) unsanitary**: be unclean, not safe

WORD PRACTICE

Fill in the correct word.

1. Americans thought that Koreans had_____to the tragedy.
2. Their reaction seemed very_____to Americans.
3. Dozens of people were____by the mass murderer.
4. The fact that he was born in Korea was_____.
5. Koreans expected a____from Americans but it never happened.
6. Frightened Korean shopkeepers_____up their stores.
7. Some say that Koreans are too____about what others think of them.
8. It was an event they really wanted to___behind them.
9. The western media isn't used to having its hands____.
10. Americans didn't care about the killer's____background.

a. bizarre
b. paranoid
c. massacred
d. put
e. irrelevant
f. backlash
g. boarded
h. ethnic
i. tied
j. overreacted

Answers on page 160.

DISCUSS

1. Were Koreans correct to accept responsibility for the Korean-American who committed a mass murder in the USA? Should Korea be blamed when Korean citizens commit crimes in foreign countries? Why or why not?
2. What is the main reason why Koreans should NOT feel responsible for the actions of the killer?
   a. He grew up in America, not Korea.
   b. Koreans can't control what Koreans do in foreign countries.
3. Americans didn't blame Koreans for the crime of a Korean-born killer, but how about if the situation were reversed—an American killing 32 Koreans? Would Koreans blame all Americans, as the Korea Times suggested?
4. Why do Koreans worry so much about what foreigners think of them? Do you think they worry more about their image abroad than people in other countries do, or do people in all countries worry just as much as Koreans do? Tell why you think so.
5. Koreans were very surprised that there was no backlash in the US after the mass killing. Did Koreans learn a lesson from that? Will it change the way they will behave in the future or will they react the same way when the next tragedy occurs?
6. What do you think of the measures that the Korean government took during the Seoul Olympics? Consider each of the following—good idea or foolish? Tell why you think so.
   a. Making soldiers wear regular clothes
   b. Disguising military bases as companies
   c. Closing dog meat restaurants
   d. Removing street vendors
7. During international sporting events held in Korea, should the foreign news media be prevented from making reports on certain things, or should they be allowed to go wherever they want? Tell why you think so.
8. People who live in western countries do not approve of eating dogs. Should Koreans stop eating dogs to improve their image abroad? Why or why not?
9. Can foreigners' opinion of Koreans have an effect on the country? If so, in what way?
10. Do you personally care what people in other countries think of Koreans? Why or why not?
11. Have you visited any country where you disliked the people? If so, where and why didn't you like them?

Korean tourists abroad.

UNIT 36

North Korea's Fate

A country in the dark

Under new management. As soon as Kim Jong Il's youngest son, Jong Un, took over after his death in January 2013, the buzz in political circles was how long people guessed he would last. Could this totally inexperienced and unprepared 29-year-old take over a dictatorship in a culture where age is so important? Could older military leaders ever respect this young man enough to take orders from him?

Apparently not, because soon after Jong Un was installed as the official head of government it became known that Jong Un was just a figurehead and that the people really running the show were his 66-year-old aunt and uncle, Kim Kyong-hui and Jang Sung-taek. It seems that the dead "Dear Leader" had expected opposition to his son's taking over, so before his death he chose his sister and her husband to consolidate Jong Un's authority as leader.

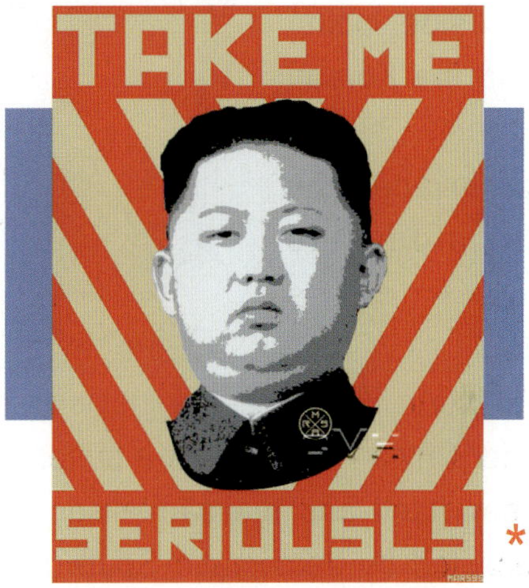

*

But that may have been wishful thinking. Jong Un's own brother, Kim Jong Nam, said, *"As a matter of common sense, a transfer to the third generation is unacceptable."* He also said he doubts that Jong Un, with only 2 years of preparation, has the ability to lead a country.

If Jong Un doesn't win the respect of the elders, a power struggle will begin.

Political

Vocabulary

- **took over**: was named as the new dictator
- **buzz**: the hot topic that everybody was speculating about
- **last**: continue, survive as leader
- **figurehead**: just for show, has no power
- **running...show**: make all big decisions.
- **consolidate...leader**: make everybody accept Jong Un as leader
- **wishful thinking**: can't really happen
- **power struggle**: several different people trying to take over the leadership

* **take..seriously:** Don't laugh, I'm not a joke.

China's role. As North Korea's only outside benefactor nation, China holds the key to North Korea's future. If the financial aid and food that it receives from China were to stop, North Korea would collapse immediately.

China is the one country that has always stood by the North's side, going back to the Korean War, when Chinese troops invaded the South alongside troops from the North.

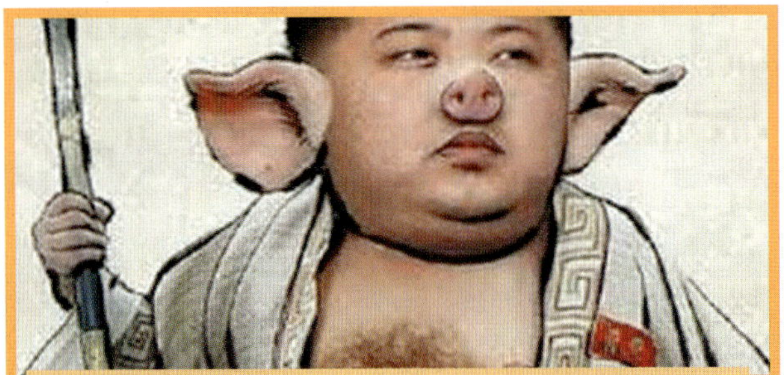

"Little Fatty" in the Chinese social media

But North Korea serves just one purpose for China—to serve as a buffer zone between itself and the capitalistic west, represented by democratic South Korea. The idea of American soldiers driving around or Americans and Japanese standing freely just across the river from China is a worst-case scenario for the Chinese government.

But China also doesn't want a nuclear war on its borders, and the North's missile testing has stretched China's patience to the limit. For the first time ever in 2013, China voted with the US, Japan and South Korea to impose sanctions against the North.

China worries that if the North is allowed to develop a bomb, the US and Japan might step up their own missile defense systems, which would be able to take out all of China's intercontinental missiles.

China's leaders are not happy with Jong Un, and it's been reported that in private they refer to him as "Little Fatty" and "Fatty the Third."

The Chinese social media has been even harsher, posting caricatures of Kim as a pig, and criticizing their own government for continuing to support the North under Kim's ridiculous leadership.

Vocabulary

- **benefactor**: gives them money and other things to support them
- **worst...scenario**: the worst thing that could ever happen in this situation
- **stretched...limit**: making them very, very angry
- **to step up**: increase
- **to take out**: destroy, eliminate
- **social media**: friendship communication websites like Facebook
- **ridiculous**: foolish, nonsensical

The technological gap is staggering.

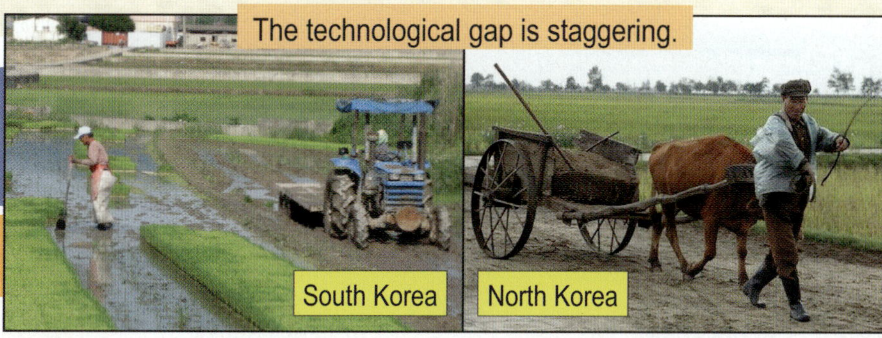

With Chinese-North Korean relations hanging by a thread and the economic and technological gaps between the North and the South growing wider everyday, North Korean escapees now living in the South scoff at the North's threats to mount another invasion.

> NK refugee: *"We all know if war breaks out, North Korea will collapse."*

When asked about the possibility of another war during yet another of the North's missile tests, a group of North Korean refugees living in Seoul all laughed. One refugee said, *"They don't have fuel. They don't have electricity. Even if they yell to the world that they'll go to war, it's all just talk."*

Another refugee said, *"It's all nonsense,"* and yet another said, *"I'm not worried at all. We all know if war breaks out, North Korea will collapse."*

Military experts say that even if North Korea has a nuclear weapon to use against the South, they'd have to truck it across the border to use it because their missiles have no nuclear warheads. If they put one on a plane, it would be shot down immediately. The North has no defense against US and South Korean air power, so any attempt to invade the South would be suicidal.

If North Korea is in such a weakened position, why don't the US and South Korea just attack and end it all? Because invading, occupying and governing the defeated North would take years and costs more money and lives than either the US or South Korea wants to spend.

A country with no future

Political

Vocabulary

- **hanging...thread**: very weak relationship, could easily break
- **to scoff (at)**: laugh at, to mock, ridicule
- **nuclear warhead**: needed to attach a bomb to a missile
- **air power**: planes and air missiles carrying bombs
- **the status quo**: conditions exactly as they are right now, no changes

WORD PRACTICE

Fill in the correct word.

1. Everybody is wondering how long Kim Jong Un will____.
2. He's just a____with no real power to make big decisions.
3. His aunt and uncle are____the____.
4. China is North Korea's sole____.
5. North Korea would collapse in a____if China's support stopped.
6. Refugees____at the suggestion that North Korea will start a war.
7. US soldiers at China's border would be a worst-case____ for them.
8. The US and Japan might____their own missile programs.
9. The____will continue for the time being.

a. status quo
b. figurehead
c. show
d. heartbeat
e. scenario
f. step up
g. last
h. running
i. scoff
j. benefactor

Answers on page 160.

DISCUSS

1. Do you agree or disagree with Jong Nam's suggestion that his brother will fail?
   a. No, he will succeed and lead the country for decades, like his grandfather.
   b. I agree that he will fail, and someone else will take over the country.
2. Will North Korean military leaders respect Jong Un as they did his father? Explain.
   a. They already respect him b. They will never respect him because…
   c. They will eventually come to respect him.
3. What do ordinary North Koreans think of Jong Un in private? Do they think he's a great leader or just a joke? Tell why you think so.
4. Who is responsible for the continuation of the harsh treatment of the citizens and the concentration camps, even after Kim Jong Il's death—Jong Un or his aunt and uncle?
5. Why does the cruel treatment of North Korean citizens go on? Why don't they close down the concentration camps? Tell why you think so.
6. What do you think best explains North Korea's development of nuclear weapons? Tell why you think so.
   a. They think they can defeat the South and make Korea communist.
   b. Self preservation. They are afraid that the rich South will overwhelm them.
7. What would China do if North Korea were to invade the South again?
   a. They would help the North fight against the US and South Korea.
   b. They would try to stop the war, they wouldn't fight.
8. What do you think of the North Korean refugees' mockery of Jong Un's threats of war? Do you agree with them? Are they right?
9. Does Jong Un and the North Korean military really believe that they could conquer the South in a war? If not, then why do they continue to make threats of war?
10. What will happen if Jong Un cannot be accepted as the real leader of North Korea? Will a power struggle begin? Is it already going on now?
11. If a new leader is chosen, marking the end of the Kim dynasty, will that make reunification more or less likely?
12. Do you agree or disagree with the view that North Korea has no future and that the only thing that can happen is that the country will eventually be absorbed by the South?
13. What's your view on reunification? Tell why you think so.
    a. It will happen soon. b. It will take 5 to 10 years. c. It will never happen.

UNIT 37 The "Comfort" Women

One of the most horrendous atrocities ever committed against human beings was a secret hidden from the world for over 50 years. In December of 1991 a group of Korean women who identified themselves as "military comfort women" filed a lawsuit against the Japanese government for violating their human rights. They claimed that they had been among the 200,000 Korean women forced to be sex slaves for Japanese soldiers during the Second World War.

The women, by then in their 60s or older, had kept silent for all those years out of a sense of shame and embarrassment. They had suffered at the hands of the Japanese military as no human beings should be made to suffer. Not surprisingly, the reaction of the Japanese government was denial. They claimed that the charges were false. They only admitted to a corps of teishintai (voluntary corps) women who cared for soldiers' needs in the field, such as washing clothes and cooking meals. That turned out not to be true.

A month after the lawsuit was filed, a Japanese history teacher discovered WWII military documents that exposed the Japanese government's lie. There was no more denying the past crimes of the Japanese government toward Korean women.

Korean women made up about 85% of the sex corps, with the remaining 15% being Chinese and Filipino.

In the years that followed it became clear that Korean women made up about 85% of the sex corps, with the remaining 15% being Chinese and Filipino.

A "comfort" station: sex time limit: 20 minutes.

Political

Vocabulary

- **horrendous**: extremely terrible
- **atrocities**: terrible things done to people
- **filed...lawsuit**: sued in the court of law
- **suffered...military**: the military made them suffer
- **voluntary corps**: group of people who performed their duties willingly

Japanese soldiers lined up to have sex.

The documents found by the history teacher proved the existence of a large-scale system set up specifically to provide sex for soldiers. The government's reasoning at the time was to build morale among the troops by providing them with sex whenever they wanted it. Another reason given was to prevent the spread of sexually transmitted diseases.

The teacher's findings were printed in one of Japan's major newspapers, forcing the Japanese government to admit the truth. In the years that followed this amazing revelation, more horrid details came out about the ordeal the women had been forced to undergo.

Girls as young as 14 years old were kidnapped from their villages or schools and thrown into trucks. The young girls were then taken to cargo ships bound for military bases in China, where they were thrown into brothels and forced to have sex with 40 or 50 men a day. Each soldier paid a fee for 15-20 minutes of sex, and the fee depended on their rank.

"Each woman was forced to have sex with 40 or 50 men a day."

Girls who refused to have sex or who tried to escape were crippled so that they couldn't run away. Girls who got sick and could no longer have sex were killed.

Girls who got pregnant and had babies were forced to have sex immediately after giving birth, and their babies were killed. What happened to these women was so despicable that the Japanese government simply can't bring itself to admitting publicly that it ever happened.

Comfort women being delivered to their comfort stations.

Political

Vocabulary

- **build...troops**: keep them happy
- **sexually...diseases**: diseases that are passed on through having sex
- **revelation**: be victims of mind control
- **to undergo**: to experience, have to go through
- **brothels**: houses for having sex
- **(be) crippled**: be beaten so that they cannot walk, have their legs broken
- **despicable**: extremely terrible

Some of the atrocities committed against the girls are impossible to even imagine. One former comfort woman said that she had been forced to drink soup made from the severed heads of two girls who had been murdered for refusing to cooperate. After Japan lost the war in 1945 most of the girls were thrown into ditches and shot. The rest were just abandoned and left to die. Every woman who survived the ordeal suffered permanent physical and emotional damage.

To their credit, most of the worst details of this horrendous 13-year nightmare—from 1932 to 1945—were uncovered and made public by Japanese citizens, not by Koreans. As news of this event made its way into the global media, the outrage grew louder, and in December of 2001 the Women's International Criminal Court for War Crimes Tribunal in the Hague, Netherlands found the Japanese government "guilty of rape approved by the nation."

It stretches the imagination to think that any government could show so little respect for human life.

"They want an official apology from the Japanese government for ever allowing it to happen."

In 2007, after years of Japan's official denial of the existence of the wartime brothels, something very close to an apology came from the mouth of Japanese Prime Minister Shinzo Abe. He said the Japanese government felt "responsible" for forcing young women to work in the brothels. But that didn't satisfy the former sex slaves. They want an official apology from the Japanese government for ever allowing it to happen, not just one man's personal regrets.

This issue continues to cause many Asians, especially the Chinese, to distrust the Japanese and prevent truly friendly relations. In China, former sex slaves are demanding not just an apology but also reparations.

Demonstration outside the Japanese embassy in Seoul.

Two WWII soldiers apologized for gang raping young women.

Vocabulary

- **severed**: cut off
- **ordeal**: terrible experience
- **To...credit**: they deserved to be praised for their actions
- **(be) uncovered**: revealed
- **rape**: to force another person to have sex
- **stretching...imagination**: extremely hard to even imagine
- **reparations**: money to be paid to the victims
- **gang...women**: many men having sex with the same woman

WORD PRACTICE

Fill in the correct word.

1. Japanese treatment of comfort women was truly____
2. Some former comfort women filed a____against the Japanese.
3. The Japanese military claimed it wanted to build____among the troops.
4. The women had to____a horrible____ during those years.
5. Girls who refused to cooperate were____so that they couldn't run away.
6. The comfort women issue was____to the public in 1991.
7. Former Chinese comfort women are demanding____as well as an apology.
8. Some former Japanese soldiers apologized for____raping Korean, Filipino, and Chinese women and girls.
9. Women were forced to work in____having sex 40 or 50 times a day.

a. brothels
b. crippled
c. atrocious
d. revealed
e. lawsuit
f. ordeal
g. gang
h. undergo
i. reparations
j. morale

DISCUSS

Answers on page 160.

1. Has the Japanese government apologized enough for this horrible crime? If not, what more should they do?
2. Who should be blamed the most for what happened to the comfort women during and before World War II? Tell why you think so.
   a. The Japanese government
   b. The Japanese military
   c. The Japanese people
3. Do you think that ordinary Japanese people in the 1930s and 1940s knew about the comfort women? If not, would they have approved of it? Could they have done anything to stop it? Why or why not?
4. Most of the details about the comfort women were discovered and revealed by Japanese people, not Koreans. Does that prove that today's Japanese people respect Korean people more? Why or why not?
5. Is it fair to blame today's Japanese people for the sins of their grandfathers? Tell why you think so.
6. What do you think about Japan in general? Why do Koreans and Japanese still have a bad impression of each other 70 years after the occupation ended?
7. Will the Japanese government ever apologize to the Asian people for their war crimes? If not, will they ever be liked?
8. Many Asians, particularly the Chinese, don't trust the Japanese because of what they did during the war that ended 70 years ago. What would the Japanese have to do in order to end that distrust, or will it never end? Tell why you think so.
9. In 2011 Korean police arrested 8,000 people for human trafficking forcing women from SE Asia, Russia, and other poor countries into sexual slavery. Isn't this the just the same as what the Japanese did to the comfort women? Why or why not?
10. The woman in this picture is from Mongolia, and she's 25 years old. She was lured to Korea to study English for free but was then forced into prostitution in Jeju for 3 years. She eventually escaped. Doesn't the existence of this sex slavery in Korea make it more difficult for Koreans to complain about the Japanese treatment of comfort women? Why or why not?

Political

UNIT 38 North Korean Refugees

School for NK refugees in Seoul

Fitting in. For the thousands of North Koreans who have managed to escape to the South, fitting into South Korean society has been a challenge.

Since the death of Kim Il Sung in 1994 the number of refugees pouring into Seoul each year has skyrocketed. They are all excited to be now living in a modern "land of plenty", but their lives are anything but easy.

The biggest challenge they face coming from the poverty-stricken North where their biggest daily challenge was finding food to eat, is having to adjust to life in a wealthy, hyper-competitive society like South Korea, where so much importance is placed on a person's education.

They lack that education, so South Koreans look down on them as uneducated country bumpkins. Their lack of education qualifies them for only the lowest-paying jobs that Southerners don't want to do.

"South Koreans look down on them as uneducated country bumpkins."

Although they speak the same language and share the same heritage as South Koreans, they're treated like foreigners because their Northern accent makes them seem different and even open to ridicule.

But not all South Koreans make fun of the Northerners. More and more schools dedicated to teaching refugees how to live in the South are opening up, and the number of refugees grows by 3,000 or so every year. One of the biggest challenges that they refugees have is learning how to think for themselves. Basic education in the North is centered around teaching children to obey their dictator and hate Americans.

6-year-olds in North Korea are taught to hate Americans.

Vocabulary

- **to fit in**: become an integral part [of the society]
- **hyper-competitive**: extreme competition for getting into schools and getting a job
- **look...on**: think of them as being inferior to themselves
- **country bumpkin**: an uneducated person from the countryside, never went to school
- **heritage**: history, ancestry
- **open...ridicule**: People laugh at them [because they talk funny]
- **poor nutrition**: not enough vitamins and minerals in their food

Political

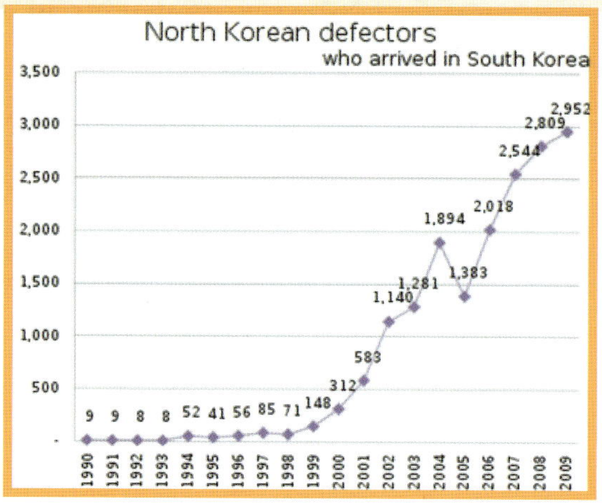

There was a lot of speculation and hope that conditions for the North Korean people might improve after Kim Jong Il died, but that hope soon faded when Jong Un started firing missiles 3 months after he was installed as leader. Nothing has improved since Jong Un took over.

Concentration camps continue, and people are still publicly executed for stealing a bowl of rice. No wonder so many North Koreans are willing to risk their lives to get out. They feel they have nothing to lose.

Most refugees get to the South by crossing the border into China and then by means of an underground railroad that runs south through China, Laos and finally into Thailand, where they are then expatriated to South Korea as political refugees. Since the end of the Korean War in 1953 over 25,000 North Koreans have found their way to the South, the number rising each year.

North Korean defectors living in Seoul are now actively involved in the underground railroad and trying to put pressure on the Chinese government to release the defectors that they are holding prisoner. Until now the Chinese have been treating defectors as illegal aliens that should be returned to their home country, but expatriating them

South Koreans' "Save My Friends" campaign in 2012 to prevent the Chinese from sending 30 North Korean defectors back to North Korea.

to North Korea is a certain death sentence for them.* International pressure on China not to return the defectors is increasing, and the people who are driving the campaign to save them are refugees now living in South Korea.

Vocabulary

**This position puts China in violation of the UN Convention Relating to the Status of Refugees, which states that no member shall return a refugee to a country where he or she is in danger of being executed.*

- **speculation**: guessing, wondering about...
- **to fade**: go away, stop hoping
- **[It's] no wonder**: it's not surprising, to be expected
- **have...lose**: even if they get killed, it's no worse than starving in North Korea
- **underground railroad**: a secret system of guiding the refugees to freedom
- **expatriated**: sent back to the country where they came from

WORD PRACTICE

Fill in the correct word.

1. The biggest problem the refugees have is____into Korean society.
2. It is the biggest____that they face when coming South.
3. They share the same____as the Southerners.
4. Their Northern accent opens them up to____by Southerners.
5. Most are short because of the poor____value of their food.
6. South Korea is a very____society.
7. There was much____about what Jong Un was going to do.
8. Refugees risk their lives because they they have____to lose.
9. The____railroad ends in Thailand.
10. China sometimes arrests escapees and____them back home.

a. challlenge
b. speculation
c. fitting
d. nothing
e. heritage
f. nutritional
g. underground
h. expatriates
i. ridicule
j. competitive

Answers on page 160.

DISCUSS

1. Do you agree or disagree with each of these statements? Tell why you feel that way.
   a. I feel sorry for them.
   b. They shouldn't do the same work as South Koreans.
   c. I am scared to be around North Koreans.
2. When you hear that North Koreans feel alone because they are avoided by their South Korean classmates, how does that make you feel? What can be done about it?
3. Seventy percent of North Korean refugees are unemployed and earn only half of what Southerners make because they don't have the skills necessary to function in a high-tech society like South Korea. What is the best solution for this situation?
   a. Require all North Korean refugees to get high-tech training.
   b. Reserve low-skilled jobs for North Koreans while Southerners do the hard jobs.
   c. There is no one simple solution to this huge problem.
4. Do you know any refugees, or have you ever met any? If so....
   a. Was your overall impression of them positive or negative? Explain.
   b. What, if anything, makes them stand out (seem different) from South Koreans?
   c. What, if anything, makes them similar to South Koreans?
   d. Do they seem like real Koreans, or like foreigners who can speak Korean?
   e. Could you work equally well with a North Korean co-worker as with a South Korean colleague? Why or why not?
   f. Could you ever become close friends with a North Korean refugee? Why or why not?
5. How many years or decades will it take for North Koreans to be fully integrated into South Korean society? Will it ever happen, and if so, when?
6. South Koreans can spot a Northerner immediately because of his or her accent. But if the child of North Koreans parents, born and raised in the South, grows up talking and looking exactly like a South Korean, will he or she still be thought of as a Northerner?
7. If you were a Northerner starving in the North, would you try to escape, even if it meant that you could be shot? Would you take the chance? Why or why not?
8. What do you think of Southerners who risk their own safety by helping North Koreans on the underground railroad—brave, foolish, crazy? Would you do it? Why or why not?
9. How much danger is there that a 2-class society will happen in South Korea—a higher class of educated South Koreans and an underclass of uneducated Northerners?

UNIT 39 US Bases in Korea

About 28,000 American troops were stationed in South Korea in 2010, and keeping that many troops in the country costs a lot of money. Most of that cost is paid by the U.S. government, but Korea also pays a share. Since Korea is now no longer poor and one of the world's biggest economies, Americans feel it's only right for Korea's share to increase. But many Koreans disagree.

In fact, if it were up to many Koreans, there wouldn't be any US bases in Korea at all. They think that paying to keep American soldiers in Korea is a waste of money and that Americans should pay for being here.

Many Koreans see having US bases in Korea as a necessary evil. They don't like having foreign troops running around their country, but they also believe that having foreign troops in the country is the only way to keep the North Koreans on their own side of the DMZ. So should Korea have to pay for that protection?

Ever since the peninsula was divided in 1945, the North has eyed the South as a prize to be won. For decades that desire to conquer the South was based on ideology. But since the 1980s the South has grown into one of the world's wealthiest countries while the North can't even afford electric lights. Given the new reality, what are the chances that this country with no cars on its roads could actually conquer the South? If the answer is zero, then why is the US military still in Korea?

Pyongyang on a normal traffic day

Political

Vocabulary

- **(be) stationed**: be assigned to, ordered to be at that place
- **feel...right**: they think that's the fair thing to do
- **if...to**: if they had the power to decide what to do...
- **necessary evil**: something that you hate but realize you need
- **eyed...won**: thought about the South as something very desirable to acquire
- **ideology**: way of thinking, i.e., communism vs. democracy

Pyongyang slums. What they don't want us to see

Ever since the end of the Korean War in 1953 the rationale for keeping American forces in Korea has been that the North's million man army would roll its tanks across the DMZ as soon as US forces withdrew. But half a century later, the probability of such an invasion taking place is around zero.

The South's GDP is now 40 times bigger than the North's, and its modern state of the art weaponry would destroy every one of the North's 1970s-built tanks before they got across the DMZ.

The North's infamous million man army is in disarray. Soldiers suffer from malnutrition and spend more time searching for food and preventing food riots than in preparing to fight. The North's tanks and planes are outdated and can't be maintained because there are no spare parts. Even if they had them, there is no fuel to operate the equipment anyway.

Chinese troops in Korean War

The North has lost its two allies which made its 1950 invasion possible. The USSR doesn't exist anymore, and China is more interested in increasing its trade with the South than invading it. Helping the North invade the South again would mean having to fight its biggest trading partners who are crucial to China's economic development.

As for the North's nuclear weapons, they can't be used. Dropping even one of them on the South would bring about a swift military response that would end up in its own destruction. Besides that, the radioactive fallout would kill North Koreans as well as South Koreans.

Dropping one would bring about its own destruction.

Vocabulary

- **rationale**: the reason given
- **probability**: the chance or likelihood that it could actually happen
- **state...weaponry**: the most modern weapons available in the world today
- **infamous**: well known for a bad reason
- **(be) in disarray**: be confused, not well organized
- **malnutrition**: suffering from lack of food
- **radioactive fallout**: the deadly radiation that is created by the bomb

Protesters demand the withdrawal of all US troops, but neither government agrees.

So the question remains: if the North has lost its capability of invading the South, and if the South's well stocked military can easily defend the country against the North's ragtag army anyway, then why are US forces still in Korea? The answer is twofold—a) strategic interest and b) economics.

Although they don't talk much about it, the US, South Korea, and Japan all see China, with its huge population, as the next possible threat to world peace. They believe that having military bases in Korea is a major deterrent to China's potential military adventurism. It's the same reason why there are still US forces in Japan decades after World War II ended.

As for the economics, the US pumps about US$5 billion dollars into the South Korean economy each year, and that's something the South wouldn't like to give up.

So in spite of the periodic demonstrations by Koreans for the pullout of US forces from their country, that's not likely to happen anytime soon.

"In spite of...demonstrations the pullout of US forces is [unlikely]."

Although US forces have been reduced from 37,000 a few years ago to just 28,000 now, the main focus has been not on pulling them out but on moving them to locations where they are less visible. The only problem is that Koreans in less visible locations don't want them there either.

Students protest against the presence of US troops in Korea.

Political

Vocabulary

- **well-stocked**: have all of the best, most modern equipment
- **ragtag**: poorly dressed and poorly equipped
- **strategic interest**: very important location
- **(be) a deterrent**: prevent a possible event from happening
- **military adventurism**: invading other countries
- **pumps**: puts, inputs, adds to
- **(be) less visible**: be in a place where there are few people to see them

WORD PRACTICE

Fill in the correct word.

1. About 27000 American troops are____in Korea.
2. Americans feel that Korea's____of the costs should increase.
3. Many Koreans see US forces here as a necessary____.
4. The North has lost its battle with the South over____.
5. The____for keeping American forces in Korea has changed.
6. The____of another ground invasion from the North is around zero.
7. The North cannot match the South's____of the____weaponry.
8. The US has a____interest in remaining in South Korea.
9. The US, Korea, and Japan believe that US forces in Korea are a____to Chinese adventurism.

a. share
b. ideology
c. probability
d. strategic
e. rationale
f. stationed
g. art
h. deterrent
i. evil
j. state

Answers on page 160.

DISCUSS

1. Who benefits more from the presence of US troops in Korea? Tell why you think so.
   a. The US benefits more.
   b. Korea benefits more.
   c. Both countries benefit equally.
2. What's your opinion of the so-called North Korean threat? Is it really a myth, just as the article says, or can they still invade? Tell why you think so.
   a. North Korea has lost its ability to invade the South again.
   b. It's still possible for the North to invade the South.
3. What's your opinion about North Korea's nuclear weapons? Why do they have them, and would they ever use them on the South? Tell why you think so.
   a. They are strictly for self defense. They are to prevent a takeover by the South.
   b. The weapons prove that they still want to conquer the South.
4. What do you think is the main reason the USA wants to keep forces in Korea—to prevent another invasion from the North or to keep China in its place? Tell why you think so.
5. What do you think is the main reason the South Korean government allows US forces to stay? Is it for protection or for the money the US adds to Korea's economy? Tell why you think so.
6. Do you agree that China is a potential military threat to Asia? Tell why you think so.
7. The US spends a huge amount of money to keep Patriot missiles and Apache attack helicopters in Korea, but the Korean government refuses to buy them. If Koreans really want the US to leave, then shouldn't they first buy the weapons? Why or why not?
8. What is the main reason why some Koreans want the US military to leave?
   a. They think they can defend themselves without US help.
   b. They don't like having foreign troops in their country.
   c. They think the US prevents reunification.
9. What do you think of the red light districts that exist around all US military bases? Does Korea need the money that those areas add to the Korean economy? Should they all be closed down? Why or why not?
10. What would happen if the US troops all pulled out of Korea? a) The North would invade. b) Japan would help the South fight against the North. c) Nothing would happen.

Military base red light district

UNIT 40

The Asian Union?

Asian countries may one day soon follow the lead of the countries of Europe and form their own economic union similar to the EU. The first step toward such a union will be taken in 2015 with the formation of the AEC, a membership of all Southeast Asian countries.

But forming an all-Asian economic community is not easy considering the huge differences in levels of development from one country to another. Asia includes very wealthy countries like Japan, South Korea, and Singapore, and very poor countries like North Korea, Laos, Myanmar and Cambodia.

> How can a country with 1.4 billion people and one with just 5.5 million be in the same economic bloc?

How could rich countries like South Korea and Japan, with annual per capital incomes above $32,000 possibly be in the same economic union as impoverished North Korea with a per capita of just $1,800 and Laos, with a per capita $3,000?

China, with its enormous size, presents another problem. How can a country with a population of 1.4 billion be included in the same economic union as Singapore with a population of just 5.5 million?

China has a GDP (purchasing power) of $6.5 billion, and if it were part of an Asian economic bloc, it would have control over 80% of the bloc's population and more than 50% of its GDP. If included in any Asian union, China would trivialize the importance of the other members. So it is clear to see that forming an economic union in Asia is no easy task.

Per capita incomes of North vs. South Korea

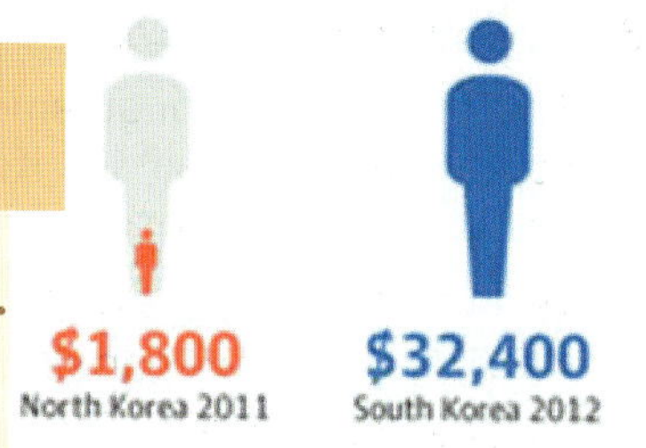

Political

Vocabulary

- **follow...lead**: do the same thing
- **EU:** the European Union, an economic trade union
- **AEC**: Asean Economic Community
- **annual...incomes**: the average earnings of all the people combined
- **impoverished**: extremely poor, doesn't have enough food or anything else
- **economic bloc**: an union of nations for the purpose of combining their economic power
- **to trivialize**: make them unimportant, irrelevant

It is easy to understand why there is so much interest in the formation of some kind of economic union. It has to do not only with the formation of the European Union but with globalization in general and the high expectations imposed on China as a future economic powerhouse. There is growing worry among the smaller Asian countries that they will eventually be swallowed up by China's massive economic machine. They think the only way they can survive is to combine forces and form a unified bloc to offset China's influence in the world marketplace.

Already 50% of the foreign investment that was going into ASEAN before 1995 is now pouring into China, and China's exports to the 5 major countries of ASEAN is increasing by 40% a year. The world's marketplace is literally awash with products made in China.

The false illusion of China's wealth. But in spite of the high level of confidence shown by foreigner investors, China is still a desperately poor country. Roughly 1 billion Chinese citizens live on less than $6 a day per family, and less than 5% live in middle-class households earning $20,000 a year.

1/3 of the Chinese live in families earning less than $6 a day...

China's socialist system, which emphasises social equality instead of individual wealth, is a drag on the country's economic development. Capitalism creates rich people; socialism is designed to do just the opposite.

So it remains to be seen whether China will actually live up to the high expectations of its worried Asian neighbors.

Chinese poverty: the world doesn't know how poor China really is.

Political

Vocabulary

- **has...with**: is concerning, is partly because of...
- **globalization**: the idea that the whole world interacts together
- **be...up**: be overwhelmed by, be overpowered by
- **combine forces**: all work together as one unit
- **(be) awash with**: have so much of
- **(be) a drag (on)**: an obstacle, makes success harder to achieve
- **to live up to**: meet its perceived ability to succeed, be as successful as expected to be

Income diversity:
A. North Korean train
B. South Korean train
C. Phnom Penh, Cambodia
D. Singapore

The desire for some kind of Asian Union isn't going to go away because the price for not doing anything is too high. At a meeting of the International Conference for Asian Political Parties (ICAPP), held in Seoul in April of 2007 four hundred delegates from 36 Asian countries adopted the Seoul Declaration which called for, among other things, the formation of an Asian Union. However, China was a party to the declaration, and it's unclear whether an economic bloc that includes China could work, because of its size.

The biggest stumbling block in the formation of an Asian Union is the inequality of its members. For a unified economic bloc to function well, all the members should be somewhat equal in population and economic potential. That was true in Europe, but it is not true in Asia.

Income diversity like this precludes the formation of an all-inclusive Asian Union like the EU. But considering the fear and distrust on the part of China's neighbors about being swallowed up, it's fairly likely that some kind of Asian union will be formed sooner or later.

Political

Vocabulary

- **the...high**: they will suffer economically if they don't do anything
- **adopted**: agreed on
- **be a party to**: participated in
- **stumbling block**: difficult problem that prevents action
- **economic potential**: have the possibility of great economic success
- **preclude**: prevent from happening
- **all-inclusive**: to include every one of them

WORD PRACTICE

Fill in the correct word.

1. The idea of an Asian____union has been____around for years.
2. One fear is that China's huge size might____the other members.
3. In an Asian economic____China would comprise 50% of its____.
4. Asian countries have high____of China's economic ability.
5. Smaller countries are in fear of being____up by China.
6. China's social system is a____on its economic development.
7. No one knows if China can____up to its expectations.
8. Income diversity____the formation of an all-inclusive Asian union.
9. It's a major____block in the formation of a union.

a. trivialize
b. live
c. bloc
d. drag
e. economic
f. stumbling
g. precludes
h. batted
i. swallowed
j. GDP

Answers on page 160.

DISCUSS

1. Do you think there is a danger that China could someday swallow up the smaller nations in Asia? Tell why you think so.
   a. Definitely. No neighboring country can defeat a country the size of China.
   b. No danger. China is poor and its potential is overrated (exaggerated).
2. Do you think that China's socialist system of government might prevent China from achieving its full economic potential, which is better acquired through capitalism?
3. What is China's main obstacle in achieving economic success? Tell why you think so
   a. its socialist / communist system of government
   b. its huge (uncontrollable) population
   c. the extreme poverty of its people
   d. distrust on the part of its neighboring countries

China's 1 billion rural poor.

4. Which of the following possible groups of countries do you think would make the best sense for an Asian Union?
   a. Korea, China, and Japan.
   b. The richest 5 or 6 countries in Asia except China.
   c. All the countries in the Pacific rim including China.
   d. All the countries in the Pacific rim except China.
5. How necessary do you think it is that some kind of Asian economic Union be formed? Is it important? Why or why not?
6. How would you feel about a United States of Asia, as one country, similar to the United States of America? Some people think that it will probably eventually happen in Europe. Would you like to see Korea as just one state of a large Asian country? Could it happen? Why or why not?
7. What do you think is the best reason for the formation of an Asian Union? Tell why you think so.
   a. To form an economic bloc to counter the USA and the European Union.
   b. To prevent Asia's economy from being dominated by China.
8. What would you think of a unified Asian currency, similar to the European Euro? Would you be willing to give up the Korean won in favor of an Asian currency? Why or why not?

Word Practice Answers

Page 4
1. D
2. A
3. J
4. I
5. H
6. G, C
7. F
8. E
9. B

Page 12
1. E
2. A
3. J
4. C
5. B
6. I
7. F, D
8. G

Page 20
1. I, F
2. B
3. A
4. J
5. D
6. C
7. H
8. E, G

Page 24
1. E
2. B
3. J
4. D, A
5. H
6. C
7. I
8. F
9. G

Page 28
1. J
2. A, E
3. C
4. B
5. G
6. I
7. D
8. H
9. F

Page 32
1. J
2. A
3. E
4. B
5. H
6. D
7. G
8. C
9. I, F

Page 36
1. A
2. E, C
3. H
4. B
5. I
6. J
7. D, F
8. G

Page 40
1. I
2. G
3. C, B
4. J
5. D
6. F
7. E
8. H

Page 44
1. E
2. I
3. A
4. G
5. C
6. B
7. J
8. H
9. F, D

Page 48
1. H
2. D, E
3. A
4. J
5. B
6. I
7. F
8. C
9. G

Page 52
1. J
2. F
3. H
4. B
5. I
6. A
7. D
8. E
9. G

Page 56
1. D
2. H
3. J
4. F
5. I, C
6. E
7. B, G
8. A

Page 60
1. B
2. G
3. A
4. I
5. F
6. C
7. J, E
8. D
9. H

Page 64
1. H
2. D
3. F
4. B
5. A, J
6. C
7. I
8. E
9. G

Page 68
1. G
2. D
3. J, H
4. B
5. E
6. A
7. C
8. I
9. F

Page 72
1. E
2. A
3. G
4. B
5. I
6. H
7. D
8. C
9. F

Page 76
1. F
2. I
3. C
4. J
5. G, A
6. B
7. E
8. H
9. D

Page 84
1. J
2. B
3. F
4. A
5. E, I
6. H
7. D
8. C
9. G

Page 88
1. A
2. H
3. B
4. E
5. J
6. I, F
7. G
8. C
9. D

Page 92
1. G
2. B
3. J
4. A
5. I, E
6. D
7. F
8. H
9. C

Page 96
1. F
2. A, I
3. J
4. D
5. C
6. H
7. G
8. B
9. E

Page 100
1. A
2. J, E
3. B
4. C, F
5. D
6. H
7. I
8. G

Page 104
1. H
2. C, A
3. J
4. I
5. E, B
6. D
7. G
8. F

Page 108
1. F
2. D
3. A
4. C, B
5. J
6. I
7. E
8. H
9. G

Page 112
1. A
2. D, G
3. I
4. J
5. B
6. E
7. H
8. F, C

Page 116
1. G, I
2. A
3. D
4. H
5. B
6. C, J
7. F
8. E

Page 120
1. G
2. D, A
3. J
4. B
5. I
6. F
7. H
8. E
9. C

Page 124
1. J
2. F
3. B
4. H
5. I
6. A
7. D, G
8. C
9. E

Page 128
1. G, F
2. H
3. A
4. J, C
5. E
6. I
7. B
8. D
9. G

Page 136
1. J
2. G
3. A, I
4. H
5. D
6. B
7. E
8. F
9. C

Page 140
1. J
2. A
3. C
4. E
5. F
6. G
7. B
8. D
9. I
10. H

Page 144
1. G
2. B
3. H, C
4. J
5. D
6. I
7. E
8. F
9. A

Page 148
1. C
2. E
3. J
4. H, F
5. B
6. D
7. I
8. G
9. A

Page 151
1. C
2. A
3. E
4. I
5. F
6. J
7. B
8. D
9. G
10. H

Page 155
1. F
2. A
3. I
4. B
5. E
6. C
7. J, G
8. D
9. H

Page 159
1. E, H
2. A
3. C, J
4. B
5. I
6. D
7. B
8. G
9. F